WOODEN CLOCKS

The Best of **SCROLLSAW**
Woodworking & Crafts Magazine

WOODEN CLOCKS

31 Favorite Projects & Patterns

From the editors of *Scroll Saw Woodworking & Crafts*

FOX CHAPEL
PUBLISHING

© 2009 by Fox Chapel Publishing Company, Inc.

Best of Scroll Saw Woodworking & Crafts: *Wooden Clocks* is an original work, first published in 2009 by Fox Chapel Publishing Company, Inc. The patterns contained herein are copyrighted by the authors. Readers may make copies of these patterns for personal use. The patterns themselves, however, are not to be duplicated for resale or distribution under any circumstances. Any such copying is a violation of copyright law.

ISBN 978-1-56523-427-7
Photo on page 2: The Lang Clock, by Dale Helgerson, page 137.

Publisher's Cataloging-in-Publication Data

Wooden clocks : 31 favorite projects and patterns. -- 1st ed. -- East

Petersburg, PA : Fox Chapel Publishing, c2009.

p. ; cm.

(The best of Scroll saw woodworking & crafts)

ISBN: 978-1-56523-427-7

Compiled by the editors of "Scroll saw woodworking & crafts."

1. Clocks and watches--Patterns. 2. Shelf clocks--Patterns.

3.Wall clocks--Patterns. 4. Jig saws-- Patterns. 5. Woodwork--

Patterns. I. Title. II. Series. III. Title: Scroll saw woodworking &

crafts.

TT197.5.C56 W66 2009
745.51/3--dc22   2009

To learn more about the other great books from Fox Chapel Publishing, or to find a retailer near you, call toll-free 800-457-9112 or visit us at *www.FoxChapelPublishing.com*.

Note to Authors: We are always looking for talented authors to write new books in our area of woodworking, design, and related crafts. Please send a brief letter describing your idea to Acquisition Editor, 1970 Broad Street, East Petersburg, PA 17520.

Printed in China
First printing: June 2009
Second printing: February 2011

Table of Contents

What You Can Make

Little Dutch Windmill Clock
Page 14

King of the Jungle
Carousel Clock Page 19

Treble Clef Clock
Page 24

Keepsake Trinket Boxes
Page 26

The Pendulum Heart Clock
Page 30

"I Love Golf" Clock
Page 32

Elegant Fretwork
Page 34

Sports Wall and Desk Clocks
Page 37

Violin Clock
Page 42

A Valentine's Day Gift
Page 46

Oval Wall Clock
Page 49

Puzzle Clocks
Page 52

Patriotic Clock
Page 57

Miniature Grandfather Clock
Page 60

Cat Lover's Clock
Page 64

Woven Box Clocks
Page 69

Lizard Desk Clock
Page 73

Simple Shaker Clock
Page 74

Watchful Leopard Clock
Page 82

Romantic Stained-Glass Clock
Page 86

Fretwork Shelf Clock
Page 90

Gingerbread Wall Clock
Page 96

Japanese Mantel Clock
Page 102

Windmill Clock
Page 112

Wooden Gear Clock
Page 120

"In Flight" Waterfowl Clock
Page 134

The Lang Clock
Page 137

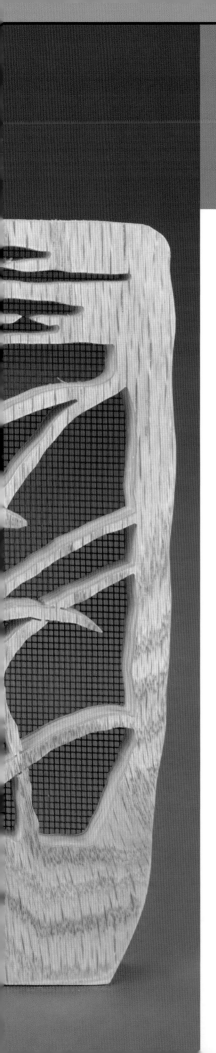

Introduction

Scroll Saw Woodworking & Crafts is proud to present this collection of 31 clocks hand-selected from 8 years of the #1 magazine for scroll saw woodworkers. In addition to patterns, you'll find tips and techniques for cutting, finishing, and assembling, as well as inspiration for designing your own timepieces.

For your convenience, we've broken the projects down into sections according to skill level, including beginner, intermediate, and master clocks. Choose a project that suits your current abilities or build your skills by working your way up to the more advanced projects.

Handmade clocks make wonderful gifts and are popular items at art and craft fairs. Whether you're making an heirloom clock to be handed down through generations or building inventory for your next show, you're sure to find dozens of designs to keep you making sawdust.

"In Flight" Waterfowl Clock,
by Tim Andrews, page 134.

A Note about Scroll Sawing Basics

If you're new to scrolling, read through the information here before you actually begin at your saw.

Safety. Though the scroll saw is a relatively safe tool, take the time to make sure you're working safely. Check that your work area is clean, well lighted, well ventilated, and uncluttered. Wear some type of safety goggles just in case a piece of wood should break free and fly toward your face and eyes. Remove any loose clothing or jewelry before you operate the saw. Don't work while you are tired, and, of course, keep your hands and fingers a safe distance away from the blade.

Tools. Gather your tools before you begin so that everything is close at hand. The projects here list the general tools that you'll need and often give other suggestions and options. Remember that the lists are simply guidelines and that you should always work with tools you feel comfortable using.

Squaring the blade. Before you begin any cutting, always check that your blade is square, or 90° to the scroll saw table. This will ensure that your cuts are accurate.

Stack cutting. This technique of simply adhering together and cutting more than one piece of wood at the same time can save you time and effort. It can also ensure a better fit for identical pieces. Pieces of wood can be held together with double-sided, painter's, or masking tape around the edges, or nails tacked into the waste areas of the wood. If you use nails, be careful that the ends of the nails do not poke through too much and scratch your saw table. If they do poke through, you can use a hammer or sandpaper to make them flush with the bottom of the stack.

Familiarize yourself with the project. It's always a good idea to read through the instructions before you begin to make sure that you understand everything that's involved.

Gather your tools before you begin so that you're sure you have everything you need and that the items are accessible.

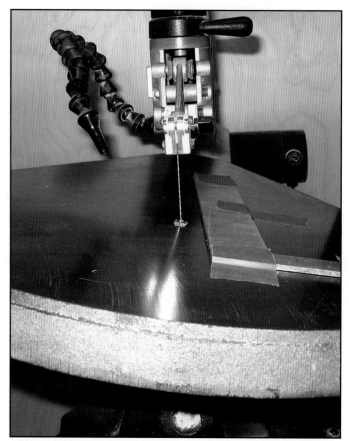

Always check that the table is 90° relative to the blade. This table and blade obviously don't form a 90° angle, but some differences won't be as obvious.

Stack cutting can save you time and energy and ensure that identical pieces both fit properly and look identical.

Tips and Techniques for Clock Inserts

Because all of the projects in this book are meant to be used as clocks, all of them employ some type of clock insert (usually a self-contained clock) or clock parts (parts that can be purchased individually to better fit a project, such as hands). If you have limited experience with clock inserts and movements, read through this section before you begin.

Make sure you have a good friction fit. Clock inserts fit through friction, so it is important that you check and double-check the size of the insert and the hole as you go. Squaring the blade is important for this step because a cut that's too far off can mean having an insert that doesn't fit. The need for a friction fit is also why many of the contributors who use routers or sandpaper to round the edges of their projects warn not to round the clock insert hole. The rounding of the edge can inhibit the fit.

When you are purchasing an insert, be careful that you choose the correct insert size for your project. Also, if you choose to enlarge or reduce a project or choose to use a different insert with the same size project, make sure you make any necessary adjustments before you begin cutting.

Pay special attention to the size and fit of the clock insert as you progress through any project. Check the actual clock —don't rely on manufacturer's catalog specs.

Beginner Clocks

These clocks are great when you're starting out, and you'll always end up with an attractive finished piece. Many of them make great gifts. All of the projects featured have the information you need to complete them. For some, that can include full step-by-step instructions; for others, all you'll need is the pattern, photo, and materials list.

Elegant Fretwork,
by Sue Mey, page 34.

Little Dutch Windmill Clock

Pays tribute to a scroller's proud family heritage

By Dirk Boelman

Ralph Waldo Emerson once wrote, "Borrow the strength of the elements. Hitch your wagon to a star . . . A Hollander's wealth is estimated not by his bonds or mortgages, but by his windmills." The Dutch windmill is the pinnacle of the Hollanders' ability to harness the wind's power to grind, cut, saw, and more importantly, prevent the land from being swallowed up by the sea.

In 1909, my great grandfather Jurgen (Jerry) Boelman came to America from Holland with his wife and six of his 13 children. He was a carpenter, which is probably why my grandfather enjoyed working with wood, too, as well as my Dad, and now me!

Part of the Boelman family remained in the Netherlands, and it was only two years ago that we were re-connected when a good friend from

South Dakota searched for Boelman family members when he visited the country.

This delightful little windmill miniature clock pays tribute to the heritage and the perseverance of the Dutch people. I'm very proud of my Dutch roots, and I hope you enjoy scrolling this project as much as I've enjoyed bringing it to you.

Before you begin, it helps to decide if you want to paint the project or leave it natural. Use pine or plywood if you wish to paint or stain your project, or select contrasting colors of solid woods for their natural color and beauty. Cut the wood pieces to approximate size to make them easier to manipulate while sawing.

Photocopy the patterns at 100 percent, thus saving the originals for future use. Temporarily adhere the patterns to the wood using a suitable spray glue. The base is bevel sawn, which means that the bottom will actually be larger than the top. When affixing the pattern for the base piece, center it on the wood and allow about ½" of space all around the edges.

Materials & Tools

Materials:
- 1 piece of wood, ¾" x 3½" x 16"
- 1 piece of wood, ¼" x 5" x 12"
- Mini clock insert, 1⁷⁄₁₆" (36mm) diameter
- ¾" #18 nail or brad or a ¾" #17 brass escutcheon pin
- Temporary bond spray adhesive
- Glue
- Felt pads or dots (optional)

Tools:
- Awl
- #5 reverse-tooth blade
- ¹⁄₁₆"- and ¹⁄₃₂"-diameter drill bits
- 1⅜" Forstner bit (optional)

1 **Drill blade entry holes.** Once your wood is ready, use a ¹⁄₁₆" bit to drill the blade entry holes in the areas to be cut out of the windmill's blade sections. Placing a board under the piece will help reduce splintering on the back where the bit exits.

2 **Mark the blade centerpoint and where the blade section attaches.** Use an awl to mark these points as well as the centerpoint on the building where the clock insert will be installed. Drill a ¹⁄₁₆" blade entry hole all the way through the centerpoint on the blade. Then, drill a ¹⁄₃₂" hole (½" deep) into the blade attachment point on the building.

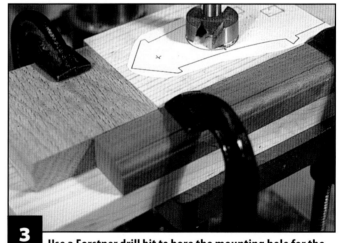

3 **Use a Forstner drill bit to bore the mounting hole for the clock insert.** You can make the hole all the way through or just ⁵⁄₁₆" deep if you don't want the opening to show on the back. If a 1³⁄₈" Forstner bit is not available, carefully scroll out the opening by keeping the blade on the inside edge of the pattern line. Test fit the clock insert, and sand or file to attain the proper fit. Clamping a couple of support blocks to a backer board under your work piece, or building some other kind of a supporting jig, will provide a much safer system for using the Forstner drill bit. These larger bits can sometimes grab and turn the wood piece out of your hands, pinching your fingers or worse!

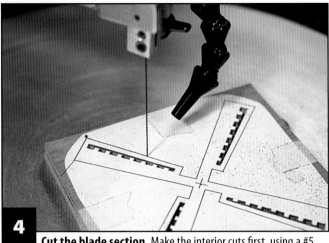

4 **Cut the blade section.** Make the interior cuts first, using a #5 reverse-tooth blade. Saw the outside contour lines last.

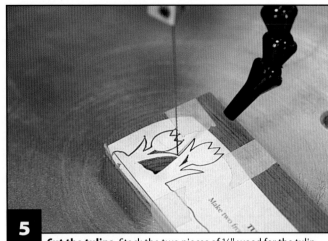

5 **Cut the tulips.** Stack the two pieces of ¼" wood for the tulip sections, and fasten them securely together with masking tape wrapped tightly around all four edges. Saw both pieces simultaneously.

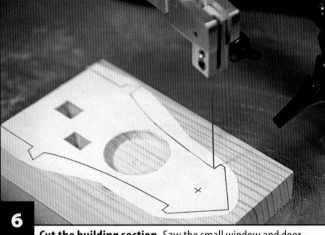

6 **Cut the building section.** Saw the small window and door openings first, along with the clock mounting hole if you are not using a Forstner bit. Cut the outside contour lines last.

7 **Scroll the base.** Start by tilting the saw table 10 degrees to the right. Saw by following the pattern lines clockwise to create the bevel-sawn edge.

8 **Retouch any parts and attach the blades.** After sawing all of the parts, touch up any imperfections with needle files, rasps, a knife, and sandpaper. Remove the paper patterns. If you wish to paint your windmill, paint the body and blades now, prior to attaching the blades. Begin by applying a sealer coat of white gesso, primer, or thinned acrylic paint. The roof and base were painted with ultramarine blue. Titanium white was used for most of the building, with a little Mars black mixed in for shadows and Mars black for inside the window and door cutouts. The blades are a mixture of yellow oxide, raw sienna, and titanium white. Once the paint is dry, attach the blades to the building with a ¾" #18 nail or brad or a ¾" #17 brass escutcheon pin.

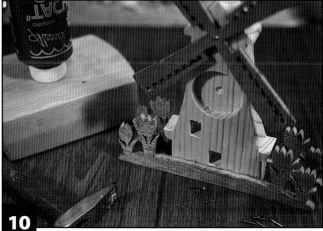

9   **Paint the rest of the parts.** Again, start with a sealer coat of white gesso, primer, or thinned acrylic paint. Use the photo on page 14 if you wish to paint your windmill like ours, which was painted by my associate, Theresa Bezdecny. The lower dividing section is a mixture of yellow oxide, raw sienna, and titanium white. Cadmium red, cadmium yellow light, cadmium orange, and dioxazine purple were used for the tulips. Thin lines of white were added to create the petals. The grassy areas, stems, and leaves are a mixture of permanent green light, pthalo green, titanium white, and yellow oxide. After everything is dry, apply a very thin line of red along the straight edges of the blade cutout areas. You can also apply a thin line of light green mixture along the leaves and top of the grass.

10   **Assemble the clock.** Stand the building upright on a flat surface. Center and glue the tulip sections to the front and back of the building. We use a tacky glue, which will bond surfaces that have already been painted and finished. Glue the upright piece, with tulip sections attached, to the top of the base on the location shown on the pattern. Insert the clock and proudly display your finished project. As a final step, you may also want to attach small felt pads or dots to the bottom of the base to prevent marring of furniture.

HELPFUL PATTERN GLUING TIPS FROM DIRK BOELMAN   **TIP**

People always ask me, "How do you know how to get the right amount of glue on the pattern?" The following method has always worked great for me.

You can make a spray booth from a cardboard box, but make sure to take it outside whenever possible to avoid fumes. Stand the box upright, and place the pattern face down in the bottom of the box. Hold the spray can approximately 6" to 8" from the paper and apply the glue in a fast circular motion, covering all parts of the paper.

While spraying, count one thousand one, one thousand two, one thousand three, and so on, up to one thousand six. Stop spraying, but continue counting up to one thousand twenty. Then, lift the pattern and adhere it to the top of the wood. Rub the surface and edges down firmly with your hands.

The additional counting time between spraying and affixing the pattern to the wood allows the glue to become a little tacky, causing it to bond better. Counting times will differ with brands of glue, size of area of coverage, and how fast or slow you count. But, after you do it this way a couple of times, you'll be able to get a perfect bond.

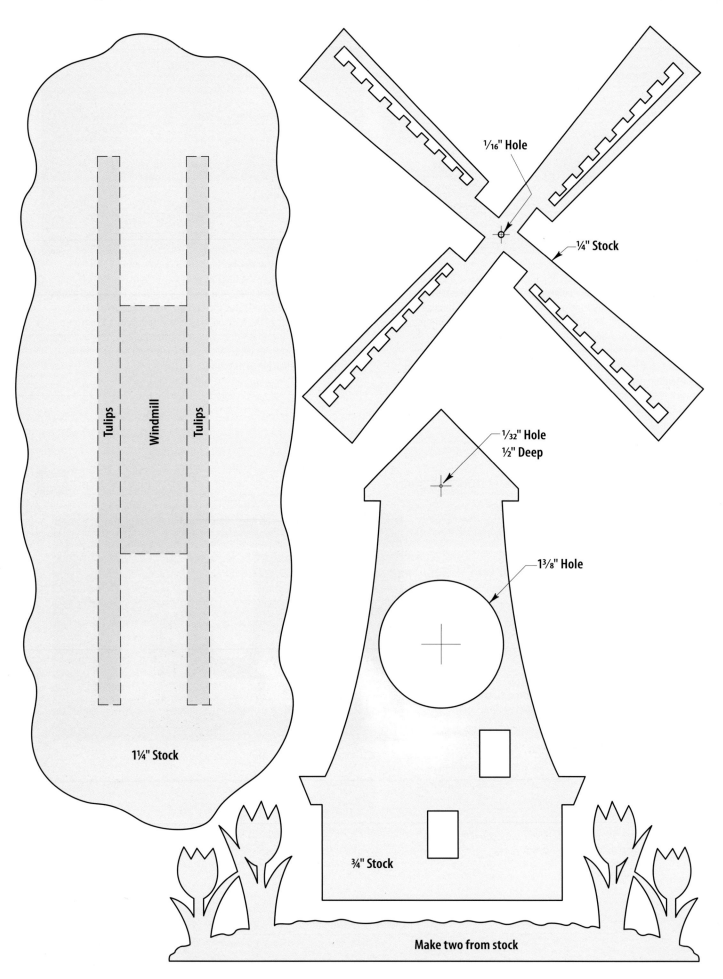

Tulips

Windmill

Tulips

1¼" Stock

¹⁄₁₆" Hole

¼" Stock

¹⁄₃₂" Hole
½" Deep

1³⁄₈" Hole

¾" Stock

Make two from stock

King of the Jungle
Carousel Clock

Recall the fun of a carousel ride with this stylish timepiece

By Paul Meisel

Who can forget their first ride on a merry-go-round? The music, the lights, the heady sensation of going around and around and around, high up in the saddle of a pretty pony or a fearsome lion. If you were lucky, you got a kangaroo to ride. My memories of carousels inspired me to create this charming clock that features the king of the jungle.

Getting Started

Carefully study each detail of the plan before starting. As you review the instructions, note the tools needed and assemble them. Next, select the wood. The front panel is ⅛", and the back panel is ¼". Birch plywood is recommended because it has a smooth surface with a tight grain. Lower-grade materials, such as fir plywood or tempered hardboard, could be substituted, but they require a good deal more surface preparation.

After attaching the pattern to the front panel, it's time to temporarily fasten the front panel to the back panel. Holding the panels together is important as you both drill the clock movement shaft and saw the outside shape of the clock. You can

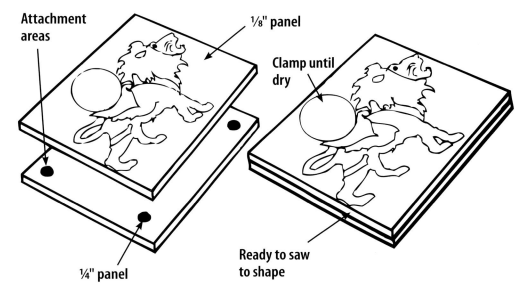

Figure 1. Attachment Positions. You can use either glue or small brads to attach the front panel to the back.

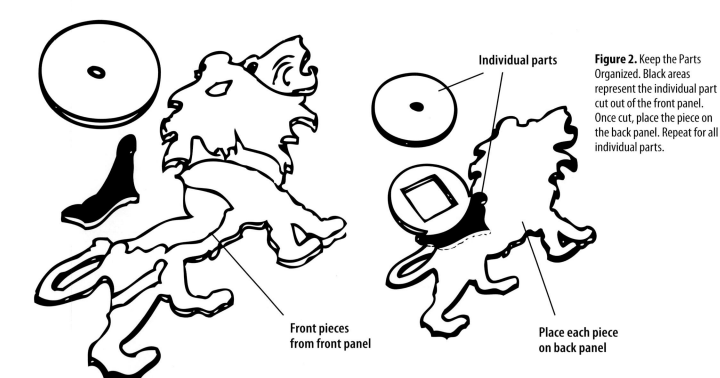

Individual parts

Figure 2. Keep the Parts Organized. Black areas represent the individual part cut out of the front panel. Once cut, place the piece on the back panel. Repeat for all individual parts.

Front pieces from front panel

Place each piece on back panel

either attach the pieces with small wire brads placed outside the lines of the pattern or by strategically placing small dabs of glue in three or four places, again, outside the pattern lines. If you use glue, use clamps to hold the pieces in place until the glue hardens (see **Figure 1**). Mark the location of the 2¹⁄₆₄" hole for the shaft of the clock movement. Using either hand or power tools, drill the hole all the way through both panels.

Cutting the Shapes

As you move to actually cutting the shapes, keep a few points in mind. The first regards blade selection. Though it's always a matter of personal preference, you may want to use a fine blade, even though the sawing may go a little slower. The resulting smooth (and easily finished) outside edges generally make it worth the extra sawing time. Also, take note that the individual pieces are NOT sawed out at this time. All you want to do is follow the outside outlines of the pattern as you saw the front/back panel combination.

After the outside shape has been cut, separate the two panels and set the front panel aside. To create a cutting line for the insertion of the clock movement, you'll want to trace around the outside of the clock movement. First, place the shaft of the clock movement into the hole you drilled in the back panel, then position it so the bottom edge of the movement is parallel to the lion's feet. Saw the square hole in the back panel.

Cutting out the individual parts from the front panel comes next. Saw each piece out of the front panel. Take your time to ensure your cuts are clean and smooth. Place the parts on the back panel as you saw them from the front panel (see **Figure 2**). Doing so helps keep the parts organized. Discard the area formed by the tail loop and the small triangle at the tip of the tail.

Next, it's time to do some sanding. You want to sand a chamfer onto the edge of each front panel part. A drum sander attachment on a drill press works very well except for on the smaller inside curves. Those curves will require hand sanding.

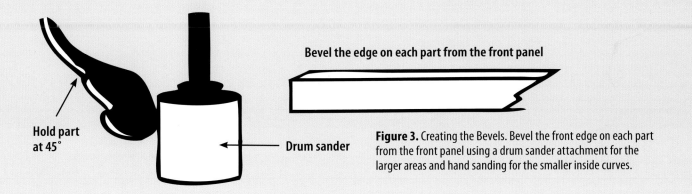

Bevel the edge on each part from the front panel

Hold part at 45°

Drum sander

Figure 3. Creating the Bevels. Bevel the front edge on each part from the front panel using a drum sander attachment for the larger areas and hand sanding for the smaller inside curves.

When using the drum sander, hold the part at a 45° angle to the sander (see **Figure 3**). After machine sanding, hand sand with 150- or 180-grit sandpaper.

Painting Comes Next

The pattern includes suggested colors, but the choice of colors is ultimately up to you. Paint the top and edges of each of the front panel pieces. On the bottom panel, paint only the edges and those areas exposed by the pieces that were discarded from the tail loop and the tip of the tail. The edges of the back panel may be painted the same color as the main body or you may wish to paint them to match the colors used on the individual pieces of the front panel.

After the first coat, lightly sand each piece, being careful not to remove too much paint. The goal is to sand just enough to knock off the irregular surface that arises when the wood swells from the moisture in the paint. Paint each piece again, or, if you prefer a very dense color, add a third coat after a light sanding with 220-grit sandpaper.

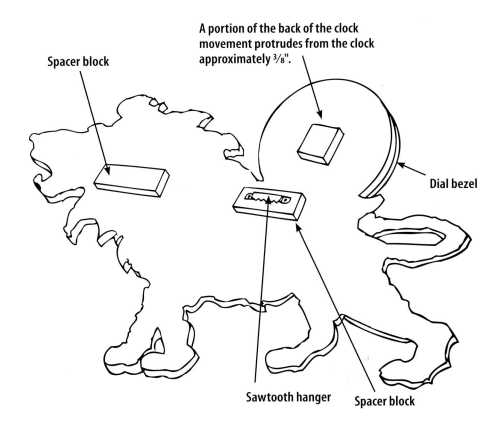

Spacer block

A portion of the back of the clock movement protrudes from the clock approximately 3/8".

Dial bezel

Sawtooth hanger

Spacer block

Figure 4. Installing the Spacers and Hanger. First, find the balance point for the hanger by holding the clock between your two index fingers, then follow the illustration for positions of the spacers and hanger.

TIME AND MONEY SAVER	TIP

Save a trip to a copy machine with this alternative to attaching the pattern to wood with adhesive: Use transfer or carbon paper. Put the paper between the pattern and the front panel with the ink side facing the wood. Fasten the pattern to the wood with masking tape to prevent slipping, then use a pencil to trace the lines of the patterns. Remember to press down as you trace the lines.

Clock movement

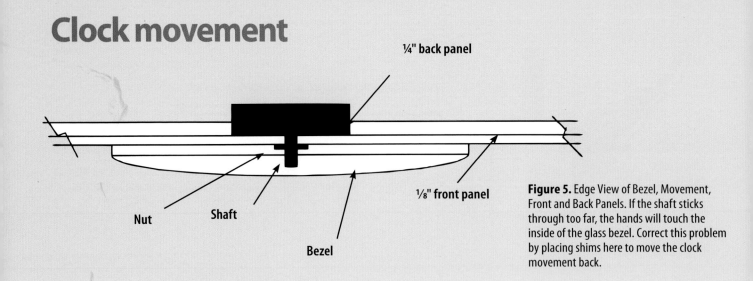

¼" back panel

Nut

Shaft

Bezel

⅛" front panel

Figure 5. Edge View of Bezel, Movement, Front and Back Panels. If the shaft sticks through too far, the hands will touch the inside of the glass bezel. Correct this problem by placing shims here to move the clock movement back.

Adding the Finishing Touches

All that remains is gluing the pieces to the back panel, attaching the eye, and installing the clock movement, dial bezel, and clock hands. The first piece to be glued should be the round piece with the ²¹⁄₆₄" hole. Continue to glue each of the remaining pieces to the back panel.

If you've chosen to use a plastic animal eye, you'll need to drill a small hole to accept the shank that extends from the back of the eye. Be sure to drill into a piece of scrap wood to test that the shank fits snugly into the hole. Drill all the way through the project and tap the eye into place. Use a soft cloth over the eye or use a rubber-headed hammer when tapping the eye into place to help prevent marring the surface of the eye.

The last things to be done all involve the clock. First, fasten the dial bezel using either small brass nails or glue. The dial bezel has a hinge on one side so it can be opened to attach the clock hands. If using glue, select an adhesive that will stick to both the wood and the metal. Silicone adhesives work well. Be sure that the number 12 is on the top, and use the glue sparingly. The clock movement helps hold the dial bezel.

Due to limited space in the bezel, you'll need to be careful that the shaft of the clock movement does not extend any further than necessary into the cavity. You may need to add spacers to position the movement back far enough so that just enough threads protrude to allow the nut to hold. The total thickness of the spacers will depend on the length of the shaft. Make the spacers from thin cardboard (the type used on the back of a writing tablet.) The hands can be slightly bent to conform to the inside curve of the glass. This may be necessary if you choose to use a second hand. You may wish to omit the second hand if you experience clearance problems.

To put the final touch on the clock, attach a sawtooth hanger. First, glue two wood spacers onto the back. **Figure 4** indicates these positions. Glue one spacer onto the back of the head. The second spacer is used to mount the hanger. Hold the clock between your two index fingers to locate the balance point. Glue the spacer with the hanger already attached into this "balance point" location. Install a AA battery and set the time.

No matter where you hang this stylish clock, it will remind everyone of the fun and laughter of a carousel ride.

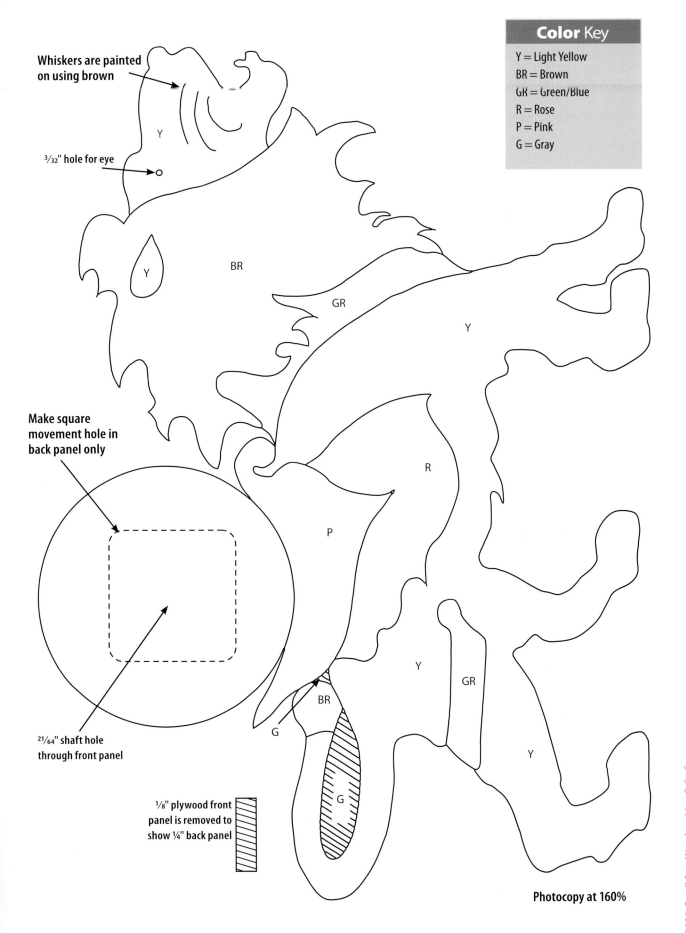

Whiskers are painted on using brown

³/₃₂" hole for eye

Y

Y

BR

GR

Y

R

Make square movement hole in back panel only

P

²¹/₆₄" shaft hole through front panel

Y

GR

BR

G

G

¹/₈" plywood front panel is removed to show ¼" back panel

Y

Photocopy at 160%

© 2009 Scroll Saw Woodworking & Crafts

Treble Clef Clock

A noteworthy gift for music lovers

By Ed Eldridge

Tasked with coming up with a theme for a gift clock to be given to my grandson's piano teacher, I was nearly out of ideas when I glanced at some sheet music. Ah-ha! That was it. A treble clef. It has just the right shape to hold a clock. I had to play around with a copier until I had an acceptable size, but it was well worth the effort. Graeme's piano teacher just loved the clock, as have others who've received it as a gift. Music lovers you know will enjoy it, too.

Materials & Tools

Materials:
- ¾" x 5½" x 17" oak
- Sandpaper, 220 grit
- Light oak stain
- Temporary bond spray adhesive
- Clear spray matte finish
- Picture hanger
- 3½" (90mm) clock movement

Tools:
- #7 reverse-tooth (11.5 teeth per inch) blades
- Drill with ⅛"-diameter bit
- Router with ¼" carbide round-over bit, brass tipped to prevent burning
- Belt sander
- Oscillating spindle sander using ¼" and ⅜" spindles

Step 1: Select the wood. For this project, you will need a nice, clear piece of ¾" x 5½" x 17" oak. Be very sure that there are no cracks in the wood because after sawing, there are parts of the design that are quite narrow. A crack at those points could be disastrous.

Step 2: Make copies of the pattern. Photocopy the pattern at right at 190% for a 17" clock. (If you would like to make a desktop version, reduce the pattern to the desired size; make sure you choose a clock insert that matches the smaller size.) Attach the paper pattern to the wood with temporary bond spray adhesive, being sure that it is secure enough not to come loose during the sawing process.

Step 3: Drill the holes. Make two ⅛"-diameter holes as shown on the plan for the inside cuts.

Step 4: Saw the pattern. Use the reverse-tooth blade recommended or one of your own choice. Feed the wood slowly and carefully into the blade, as any diversions from the line are difficult to correct later and, if left, will be magnified when routing with the round-over bit.

Step 5: Sand. After sawing is complete, check for and sand out any imperfections using the spindle sander with ¼" and ⅜" spindles. Sand the underside on the belt sander to remove any burrs.

Step 6: Check the clock's fit. Be sure that the opening for the clock insert is exactly 3". Do not round over the clock opening or the clock insert will not friction fit properly.

Step 7: Rout using the ¼" round-over bit. To avoid chip-out, make four or five passes, increasing the depth of cut with each pass, until final depth is reached.

Step 8: Final sand by hand. Use 220-grit sandpaper. Then, remove dust with a tack cloth. Apply the stain of your choice. Spray two or three coats of clear gloss or matte finish, sanding lightly between coats.

Step 9: Attach the picture hanger to the back. Drill blade entry holes for the tacks or screws. Install the clock movement. Stand back and admire the beautiful piece of work you have just completed.

LOOKS GREAT WITHOUT THE CLOCK TOO **TIP**

Insertion of the clock movement can be optional. Because it's such a well-known design, it can stand alone as a decoration, especially in the oak finish.

RESPECT THE ROUTER **TIP**

I am very respectful of the router. The further away my fingers are from the whirling bit, the happier I am. Since this is ¾" material, when the time came to rout the edge, I attached two pieces of 1½" x 1" to the back with finishing nails, which gave me a secure, safe grip on the piece while routing.

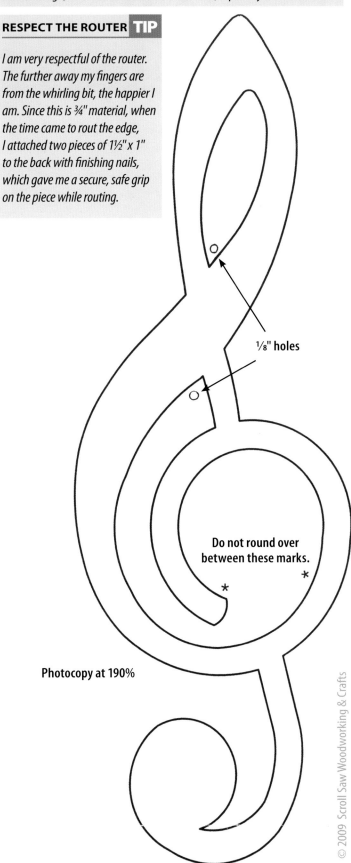

⅛" holes

Do not round over between these marks.

Photocopy at 190%

Keepsake Trinket Boxes

Materials &Tools

Materials:
- ⅛" oak (body and lid)
- ¾" oak (body)
- ¼" walnut (lid)
- ¼"- diameter x 1" wood dowel
- Masking tape
- Clock fit-up, 1⁷⁄₁₆" (36mm) bezel with 1⅜"- diameter, rear mounting
- Sandpaper, 220 grit
- Polyurethane sanding sealer
- Polyurethane clear wood finish
- Carpenter's glue
- C-Clamps
- Felt

Tools:
- Drill press with ¼"-diameter twist bit or brad point bit
- Blade of choice with 10 teeth per inch
- Reverse-skip-tooth blade with 20 teeth per inch
- Spiral blade with 41 teeth per inch
- 1⅜" Forstner bit
- Scissors
- Paper clip

Contrasting woods make them extra special

By Paul Meisel

Simple tricks, such as the use of contrasting wood, 3-D layering, and varied wood thickness, enable you to create these attractive boxes on your scroll saw. Each box features a lid that swings open on a wood dowel to reveal a hidden chamber. A clock fit-up provides the final elegant touch.

Assemble the Materials
The body of each box requires a piece of ¾" oak and a piece of ⅛" oak. The lid requires a piece of ⅛" oak and a piece of ¼" walnut.

Making the Body
To make the body, begin with a scrap of ¾" oak just slightly larger than the size of the project. For the butterfly project, I cut the oak 3½" x 6¼" long.

Next, transfer the body pattern either with transfer paper or by gluing a photocopy of the pattern directly to the wood.

For cutting ¾" oak, I use a blade with 10 teeth per inch (TPI). This blade leaves a smooth cut with no burning.

To make the bodies of the trinket boxes, begin by drilling a blade entry hole. Thread the blade and cut out only the area that will become the inside cavity. Do not cut around the perimeter at this time.

The butterfly and apple projects are both wider than 3", so if you are using the 3"-wide oak described above, you need to edge glue two pieces to achieve the required 3½" width. To edge glue, start by cutting two 6¼"-long pieces from the ⅛" x 3" x 24" piece. Rip one of these pieces to ½" width, then edge glue it to the 3" piece to get a glued up panel the same width and length as the ¾" piece. You can gently squeeze the pieces together with your fingers for a minute or two until the glue sets up, then set them aside until the glue thoroughly dries. When dry, sand off any glue squeeze-out. Finish by gluing and clamping

this ⅛" x 3½" x 6¼" glue-up to the bottom of the ¾" oak. I used C-clamps in conjunction with scraps of wood to prevent damage from the clamps.

Before the glue dries, remove any excess on the inside of the cavity with a damp paper towel. You could also use a knife point to scrape off the squeeze-out. It is easier if you begin scraping just as the glue is starting to set up.

Now saw out the outside perimeter of the project, again using the 10 TPI blade. Set the assembly aside.

Making the Lid

The lid assembly is made from ⅛" oak and ¼" walnut. Edge glue the stock as necessary depending on which box you are making. Then, transfer the respective patterns. The oak piece on top is a slightly different size and shape than the walnut piece, so each layer must be cut separately. To cut these ⅛" and ¼" pieces, I used a reverse-skip-tooth blade. This blade works well on the thinner hardwoods.

After cutting the two lid pieces, set the ⅛" oak piece aside and position the ¼" walnut on top of the body assembly. Use masking tape to hold the pieces together. They must be aligned for drilling the ¼"-diameter dowel hole. Drill down through the ¼" walnut and into the body assembly. Drill to a depth of just over ¾" to accommodate the ¾" length of dowel, which will project from the lid assembly.

Completing the Lid Assembly

Now face glue the ⅛" oak to the ¼" walnut. Be careful not to use too much glue to minimize squeeze-out.

Next drill the 1⅜"-diameter hole in the lid assembly for the clock fit-up. Use a 1⅜" Forstner bit. Drilling to the correct depth is critical. The clock fit-ups require a ³⁄₁₆"-deep hole. But since the lid is only ⅜" thick, do not drill the hole any deeper than necessary or the point of the Forstner bit will break through the bottom side of the lid assembly. The best method is to set the depth gauge on the drill press. Be sure to test the hole depth in a piece of scrap wood that is the same thickness as the lid. When the depth setting is correct, drill into the lid assembly.

The final step is to cut a 1"-long piece of ¼"-diameter dowel and glue it into the hole in the ¼" walnut. Use caution when purchasing dowels. Most hardware stores and many lumberyards use imported dowels. Imported dowels are significantly undersized and will not provide the resistance necessary for the "friction fit" required.

To finish the lid and body assemblies, start by brushing on one coat of sanding sealer. Sanding sealer is chemically formulated with a high amount of solids. Sanding sealer is designed to give a quick buildup of finish and is also formulated to sand very quickly. A light sanding with 220-grit sandpaper yields a smooth surface. Finish with a final coat of polyurethane clear wood finish.

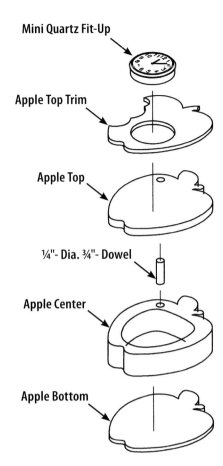

Figure 1. Assembly Drawing

Final Assembly

Redrill the ¼"-diameter hole in the body assembly if necessary to clean out any residual sanding sealer or polyurethane. Slip the dowel, which has been glued to the lid, into the hole in the body assembly. The lid is opened by rotating it either clockwise or counterclockwise (see **Figure 1**).

Cut a piece of felt the same size as the cavity. Here's my quick and easy method: Place a piece of paper over the cavity and transfer the cavity shape by rubbing with a lead pencil. This creates a temporary template. Secure the template to the felt with a paper clip. Trim the felt to size with scissors (shift the paper clip to the other side to finish the cut).

Set the time on the clock fit-up and snap it into the 1⅜"- diameter hole.

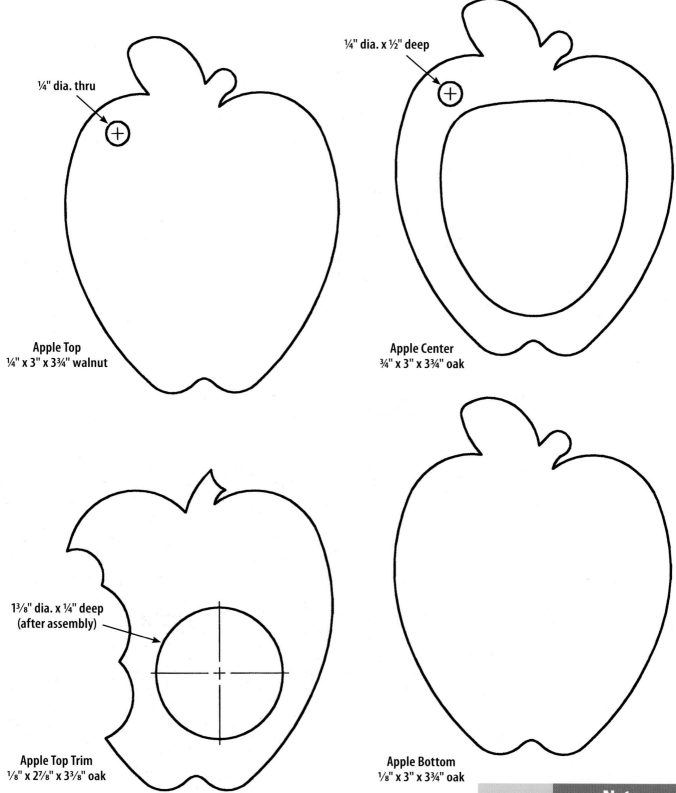

¼" dia. thru

Apple Top
¼" x 3" x 3¾" walnut

¼" dia. x ½" deep

Apple Center
¾" x 3" x 3¾" oak

1³⁄₈" dia. x ¼" deep
(after assembly)

Apple Top Trim
⅛" x 2⁷⁄₈" x 3³⁄₈" oak

Apple Bottom
⅛" x 3" x 3¾" oak

Photocopy at 100%

Note

Make two copies of this pattern. The TOP pattern is to be cut from ⅛" x 3¼" x 6" walnut. The BOTTOM pattern is to be cut from ⅛" x 3¼" x 6" oak. For the bottom, cut the outside line only and do NOT drill a ¼"-diameter hole.

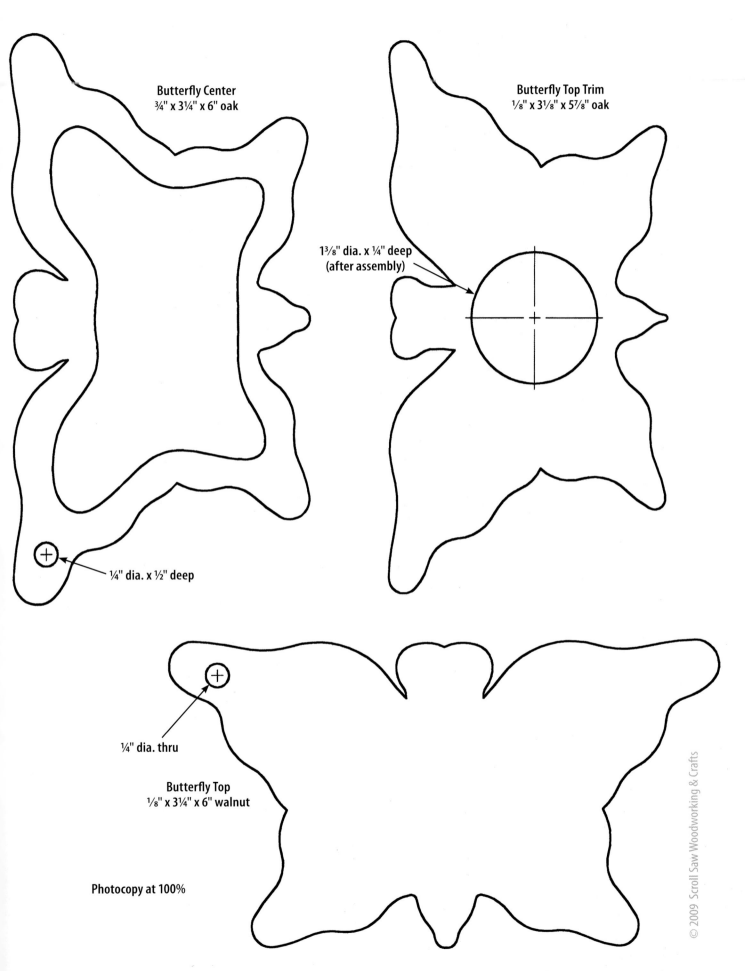

Butterfly Center
¾" x 3¼" x 6" oak

Butterfly Top Trim
⅛" x 3⅛" x 5⅞" oak

1³⁄₈" dia. x ¼" deep
(after assembly)

¼" dia. x ½" deep

¼" dia. thru

Butterfly Top
⅛" x 3¼" x 6" walnut

Photocopy at 100%

The Pendulum Heart Clock

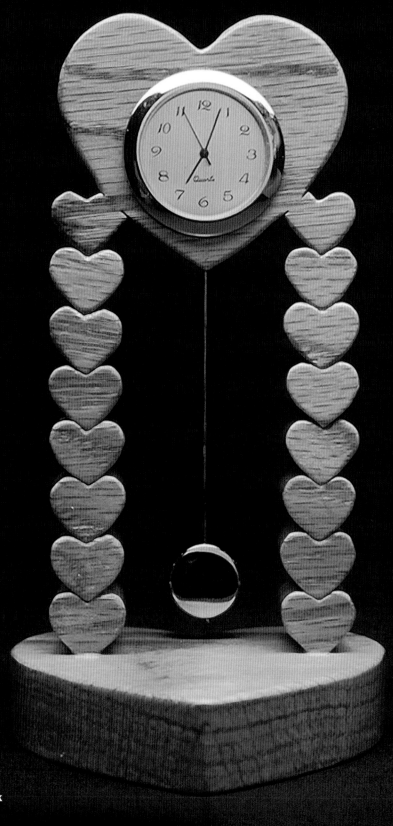

A Valentine's gift to give

By Gary Hawkes

The Pendulum Heart Clock is every scroller's dream project: It's attractive, it's inexpensive, and it's easy to make. Surprise your valentine with this unique timepiece.

Step 1 Make copies of the patterns. Keep the originals for future use. Using temporary bond spray adhesive, spray the patterns and attach them to wood.

Step 2: Drill. Using a 1⅜" Forstner bit, bore a hole through the clock block.

Step 3: Cut out all pieces using a #5 blade. You'll go through some blades, for sure, but your sanding will be next to nothing.

Step 4: Sand the pieces. Use 220-grit sandpaper to sand all pieces, knocking off all of the edges.

Step 5: Build the uprights. Using woodworker's glue, glue all the upright pieces together in a straight line. Start from the clock block and work your way down. Draw two parallel lines on a piece of paper and use them as a guide to keep the uprights straight.

Step 6: Attach the lower uprights. Glue the lower uprights to the base.

Step 7: Finish the project. Use four coats of varathane satin spray, fine sanding between coats.

Step 8: Add the clock. Install the clock insert and pendulum mechanism.

Photocopy at 125%

Materials & Tools

Materials:
- 1" x 6" x 12" red oak or wood of choice
- Wood glue
- Sandpaper, medium and fine grit
- Temporary bond spray adhesive
- Varathane satin finish spray
- 1⁷⁄₁₆" (36mm) clock insert
- Mini-pendulum mechanism

Tools:
- #5 blade
- 1⅜" Forstner bit

CENTERING A FORSTNER HOLE TIP

Draw a line from the top of the heart to the bottom of the heart. To make sure the hole is exactly in the middle, measure the length of the line and split it in half.

"I Love Golf" Clock

This easy-to-scroll project will be appreciated by anyone who hits the greens

By Diana Thompson

Seventeen years ago, my daughter asked me to go with her to a golf driving range. Neither one of us had ever held a club in our hand. She never went back, and I never left! The game has been one of my greatest joys all these years.

When things don't look so good or I get down in the dumps, the golf course is always my haven. The first two years of my woodworking career, golf took second place, and I didn't play very much. Then January 1, 2002, I made a New Year's resolution to keep my golf days no matter what was going on (translation: no matter what the editor was screaming). It's been an easy resolution to keep!

So this "I Love Golf" clock is a perfect gift for your favorite golfer and in my case, for myself. It sits on my desk as a reminder "it's time to head for the course."

This clock is easy and quick to make. It's a good way to use up those small pieces of wood left over from other projects.

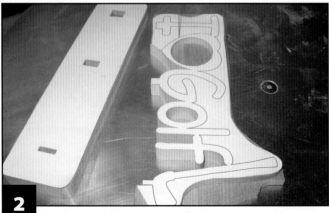

1 **Prepare your stock.** Apply each pattern to one piece of the ¼"-thick stock. Drill blade entry holes, and cut the clock opening in the upper section and the three openings in the base. Glue both pieces to the other piece of ¼"-thick stock. Clamp it into place, and allow it to dry. This method hides the back of the clock insert and gives the project a more finished look.

2 **Cut the remaining pattern on both pieces.** Drill a blade entry hole and cut out the center of the O in golf. Continue cutting the remaining pattern lines on both pieces.

3 **Apply glue to the tabs, and glue the upper section into the openings in the base.** You may need to sand the tabs a little to get them to fit into the openings on the base. Apply several coats of a clear finish. Then, snap the clock insert into place.

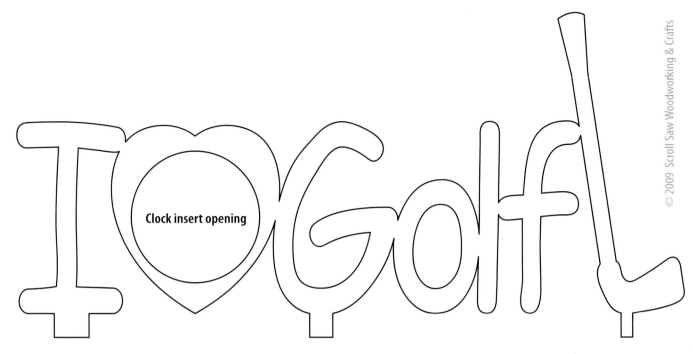

Clock insert opening

Photocopy at 100%

Base

Materials & Tools

Materials:
- 2 pieces ¼" x 6½" x 8" wood of choice (I use sycamore)
- Wood glue
- Sandpaper, 400 grit
- Wood sealer (optional)
- Clear finish of choice
- Spray adhesive
- 1⅞"-diameter (48mm) heart clock insert

Tools:
- #5 or #3 reverse-tooth blades or blades of choice
- Drill and 1⁄16"-diameter drill bit
- Several small clamps
- Scissors

Elegant Fretwork

Classic Roman clock face is easy to scroll

By Sue Mey

The fretwork portion of this project, with roman numerals and scrolls, is simple enough for a beginner to achieve good results. Paired with a simple backing board of a contrasting color, it makes a striking wall clock. The overlay can also be used to replace a store bought mechanism on more complex projects.

I use walnut stain to darken the overlay, but a dark hardwood can be used instead. Maple, beech, and light oak are all good choices for the backing.

Cut the blanks to the size listed in the materials list, then sand with 150-grit sandpaper. Sand the wood again with 320-grit sandpaper. This reduces the amount of hand sanding you need to do later; you run the risk of breaking the fragile parts of the overlay if you wait to sand after cutting.

I find I have better control if I stack cut the clock face. This provides support for the fragile areas and allows me to make several projects at once. Cover the surface of the workpiece with masking tape to allow for easy removal of the pattern after cutting. Apply the pattern to the taped surface. Use a compass to draw an 8"-diameter circle on the backing piece. Mark the center position using a punch and mallet.

This same clock face can be used on The Lang Clock, page 137, found in the Master Clocks section of this book.

Cutting and Sanding the Clock

1 **Drill the blade entry holes and cut the frets.** Use a ⅛"-diameter bit where space allows and a ¹⁄₁₆"-diameter bit for tight areas. Remove any burrs from the back by scraping with the grain of the wood. Use a #3 blade and reduce the speed when cutting fragile parts.

2 **Sand the edges of the work pieces.** After all frets are cut, cut the perimeter on the overlay and backing board with a #9 blade. Cut outside the line and use a disc sander to sand up to the pattern lines. Turn the work pieces slowly and evenly against the disc. You can also cut the circles with the scroll saw if you prefer.

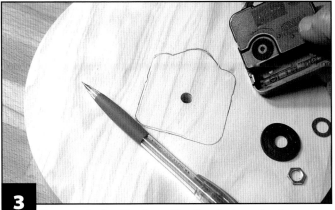

3 **Prepare the backing board for the clock mechanism.**
Drill the center hole for the quartz movement shaft, using the corresponding bit for your shaft diameter. Place the movement in position on the rear of the backing board, and draw the outline with a sharp pencil.

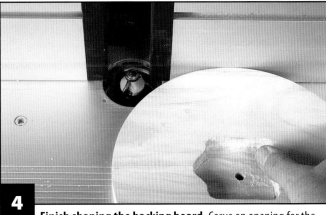

4 **Finish shaping the backing board.** Carve an opening for the quartz movement. Create the recess to the proper depth so the shaft will protrude enough in the front. Use carving tools or a router to create the recess. Using a router and a round-over bit, round over the front edge of the backing board.

FINISHING THE CLOCK

5 **Remove the pattern and masking tape.** Separate the plywood layers by inserting your blade of choice between the two pieces and prying them apart. Sand the pieces by hand with 320-grit sandpaper. Switch to 500-grit sandpaper to get a smooth finish. Be careful not to catch and break any fragile pieces. Remove all of the sanding dust.

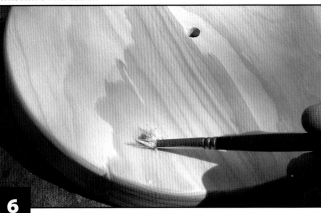

6 **Apply your finish.** Use a small paintbrush to apply deep-penetrating furniture wax liquid or Danish oil to the backing piece. Apply walnut stain to the front and side surfaces of the face. A small brush makes it easy to reach all the inside surfaces of the fretwork. Allow the pieces to dry, and wipe all of the surfaces with a dry, lint-free cloth.

7 **Glue up the clock.** Line up the clock face with the recess on the back. Apply small beads of wood glue to the back of the clock face piece. Position it on the backing board, and clamp it in place. Remove any glue squeeze-out with a toothpick. When dry, apply several thin coats of clear spray varnish.

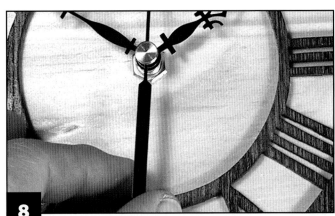

8 **Finish assembling the clock.** Attach a sawtooth hanger to the back. Place the quartz movement in position, and tighten the nut in the front. Insert the clock hands onto the shaft: first the hour, then the minute, and finally the second hand. Insert a battery, and set the correct time.

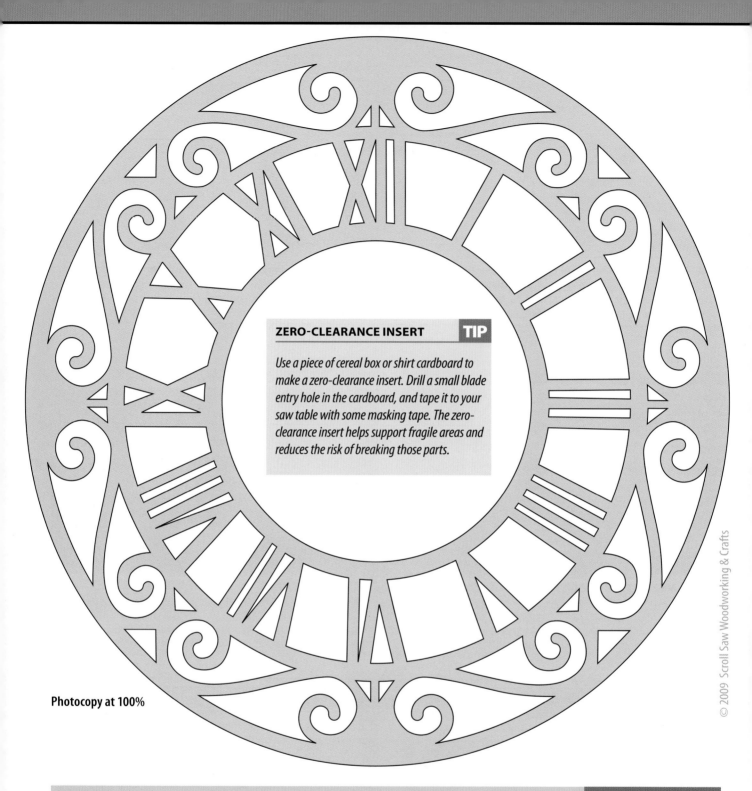

ZERO-CLEARANCE INSERT `TIP`

Use a piece of cereal box or shirt cardboard to make a zero-clearance insert. Drill a small blade entry hole in the cardboard, and tape it to your saw table with some masking tape. The zero-clearance insert helps support fragile areas and reduces the risk of breaking those parts.

Photocopy at 100%

Materials & Tools

Materials:
- 1" x 9" x 9" light-colored hardwood of choice (backing)
- ⅛" x 8" x 8" Baltic birch plywood or hardwood of choice (overlay)
- Masking tape
- Spray adhesive
- Thin, double-sided tape (optional)
- Sandpaper, assorted grits
- Wood stain, walnut (optional)
- Deep-penetrating furniture wax liquid or Danish oil
- Lint-free cloth
- Wood glue
- Clear spray varnish
- Sawtooth hanger
- Quartz movement and hands

Tools:
- #3 and #9 reverse-tooth blades or blades of choice
- Drill press with 1/16"-, ⅛"- and 5/16"-diameter bits (size of the larger bit may vary to match the shaft diameter of quartz movement)
- Disc sander and palm sander
- Router with round-over bit
- Punch and mallet
- Sharp pencil
- Clamps, assorted sizes
- Assorted paintbrushes of choice to apply the finish

Sports Wall and Desk Clocks

RED RIVER VALLEY RAIDERS
2004-2005

Use the patterns provided to make two versions of clocks: one you hang on the wall, such as the one above, or a desk sitter version. Samples of desk sitters are on page 38.

Attractive hardwood frames show off treasured photos

By Tom Mullane

Memorable photos from the Big Game or from a championship team deserve special treatment. These two simple clock frames make wonderful displays for these treasured mementos. Your favorite athlete or team sponsor will enjoy receiving this as a gift, and it is a terrific seller at craft shows, regardless of what sport season is in full swing.

Materials & Tools

Materials:

- ½" x 6" x 8" hardwood of choice (desk clock)
- 2 pieces, 1½" x 2½" hardwood same thickness of stock used for desk clock (feet of clock)
- ½" x 8" x 11" hardwood of choice
- Sandpaper, assorted grits
- ³⁄₁₆"-diameter dowel (desk clock only)
- Masking tape
- Temporary bond spray adhesive or 8½" x 11" full-size self-stick labels
- Danish or tung oil finish
- 1⁷⁄₁₆"- (36mm) or 2" (50mm)-diameter clock fitting (desk clock)
- 60mm (2⅜") clock insert and 2" (50mm) photo frame (wall clock)
- Picture mounting clips (optional)

Tools:

- #2 reverse-tooth or #1 or #3 spiral blades
- Drill with appropriate-size bit for blade clearance
- Forstner bit to match the insert size
- Palm sander or sanding block
- Tacky glue

Step 1: Prepare the pattern.
Reproduce the pattern on a copy machine or scan it into your computer. If scanning, you can change the color to make it easier to follow. Pale blue or red help because the blade stands apart from the pattern line.

Step 2: Prepare the wood.
Sand the wood before applying the pattern. Generally, you do not have to sand to any finer than 320 grit. Cover the wood with cheap masking tape. You're going to attach the pattern to the tape, so you need only cover the top surface of the wood. Why tape? It allows the blade to cut without burning, and it makes pattern removal a breeze.

Step 3: Apply the pattern and drill holes. Use temporary bond spray adhesive to adhere the pattern to the masking tape. Another alternative is to print the pattern on 8½" x 11" self-stick labels. I find this easier than using spray adhesive and lot less messy, and the price is not all that different.

Once the pattern is attached, drill a hole large enough to thread the blade through comfortably.

Position the holes in the large areas of blue, which will be cut out, near the cutting line in each of the sections. Doing so saves time and wear on your blade. Then, using an appropriate-size Forstner bit, drill the hole for the clock. You could cut the clock opening, but drilling does a much better job and the bits are reasonably priced.

Sand the back of the piece to remove all the breakout fuzzies from the drilling operation. Removing the fuzzies makes the piece slide easier on your saw table and also makes blade changes a lot easier because the blade doesn't get caught up in them.

Step 4: Cut out the shaded areas. Take your time and let the blade do the work, especially on thick hardwood like oak or walnut. This ensures that the insides of your cuts will be nice and smooth, especially if you use a spiral blade. Some woods have weird grain, and if you're using a spiral blade, it will try to follow it. Just keep a nice steady grip on the wood and guide it slowly as you follow the lines. Do not force the cuts, no matter what blade you're using.

I always cut from the inside to the outside of a pattern. This strategy gives me more support and a fingerhold when I get to some of the outside areas. Certain parts of the cutting will form small "islands" or hangers. I always use some masking tape to hold these back down to keep them from breaking due to the vibration of the saw or moving the piece around the table. It is also handy to have a zero-clearance insert set up on your tabletop. It can be as simple as a business card with a hole in it and taped to the saw table.

Step 5: Sand the project. With the pattern still attached, turn the project over and sand it to remove the fuzzies. A palm sander with 80-grit sandpaper works well as the first step in removing them. Let the sander glide over the piece without placing too much pressure on it. Next, dust the back and do this again with 120- and 180-grit sandpapers. You may need to do a little clean up with a craft knife used in a scraping motion instead of a cutting motion. When you are done, remember to dust and blow off all sanding dust from the back, the insides of the cuts, and the front.

Photocopy at 100%

⅜" diameter

© 2009 Scroll Saw Woodworking & Crafts

Step 6: Remove the masking tape with the pattern. Work carefully, so as not to break off any hangers or "islands." If there is a little fuzz on the front of the cutting, lightly sand with the palm sander or a sanding block with 220- to 320-grit sandpaper. At this point, I also round over all the edges of the piece by sanding lightly with my palm sander or sanding block. A ⅛" round-over bit in your router table or using a rotary tool with the router accessory works, too. DO NOT round over the bottom of the piece, only the sides and top.

Step 7: Make and attach the feet. The feet on these clocks could not be simpler. If you are going to use the picture clips, go to Step 10 before you attach the feet. They consist of two pieces of the same stock used to make the clock that measure 1½" x 2½". The top edges are rounded over slightly by sanding with a palm sander or sanding block. I like to place the feet about an inch in from the ends.

I generally attach the feet with a dowel and glue, but you might decide to use a small nail or screw instead. Either way, it is good to drill holes for whatever attachment you are going to use in both the foot piece and the clock. Make sure you plan the hole for the dowel or screw so that it will not penetrate the frame area or one of the cutouts in the sports figure. In other words, watch your depth.

If you do not have a drill press, I suggest you lay the clock on its back and very carefully drill the holes for the feet while making sure that the drill is entering the pieces squarely. This can be tricky, so go slowly. On the feet, I drill the hole centered on the foot.

If you're attaching with the dowel method, glue a precut dowel into the clock first. Then, place a bit of glue in the hole of the foot and a

little across the foot at the dowel point. Gently wiggle the foot onto the dowel and press it flush with the clock so it is perpendicular to the face. If you do this properly and the dowel is a snug fit, you will most likely not need to clamp the foot in place. Make sure the dowel is cut short enough that it does not protrude from the bottom of the foot. If you like, you can put a piece of self-stick felt on the bottom of the foot to dress it up a bit.

Step 8: Apply finish. The finish for these clocks can be just about anything you are comfortable with. I like to use either Danish oil or tung oil. Both finishes really bring out the colors of the oak and are easy to apply. Follow the manufacturer's directions on whatever finish you use. Personally, I don't care for polyurethane as a finish because it leaves a plastic look.

If you are going to use the picture clips, go to Step 10 before you complete the finishing stage. You need to lay the project face down in order to add the screws. You don't want to risk marring the finish.

Step 9: Mount the picture. At this point, you have two options for mounting the picture. You can either glue it directly to the back or add picture clips. If gluing, lightly sand the area around the frame in the back for better adhesion and put the glue on the wood away from the edge so that it does not smear into the opening.

Picture mounting clips are a good choice, too. These small clips are mounted with a small nail or screw and swivel to hold the picture in place with a piece of thin cardboard in back. If you decide to add picture clips, predrill the holes for the screws so that you do not split the wood. Be careful not to drill through the face of the piece.

Another option in the final mounting is to glue a piece of black, heavyweight, acid-free art paper to the back of the finished piece. I have done these clocks many ways and prefer the open look of no backing, but it is your clock, so you decide. If you do decide to use the black backing, make sure you cut an opening that will allow you to remove the clock and photo frame when you need to.

Step 10: Mount the clock and photo frame. They are pushed into the holes you drilled with the Forstner bit. Just make sure you align them properly and do not try to force them or break the friction tabs.

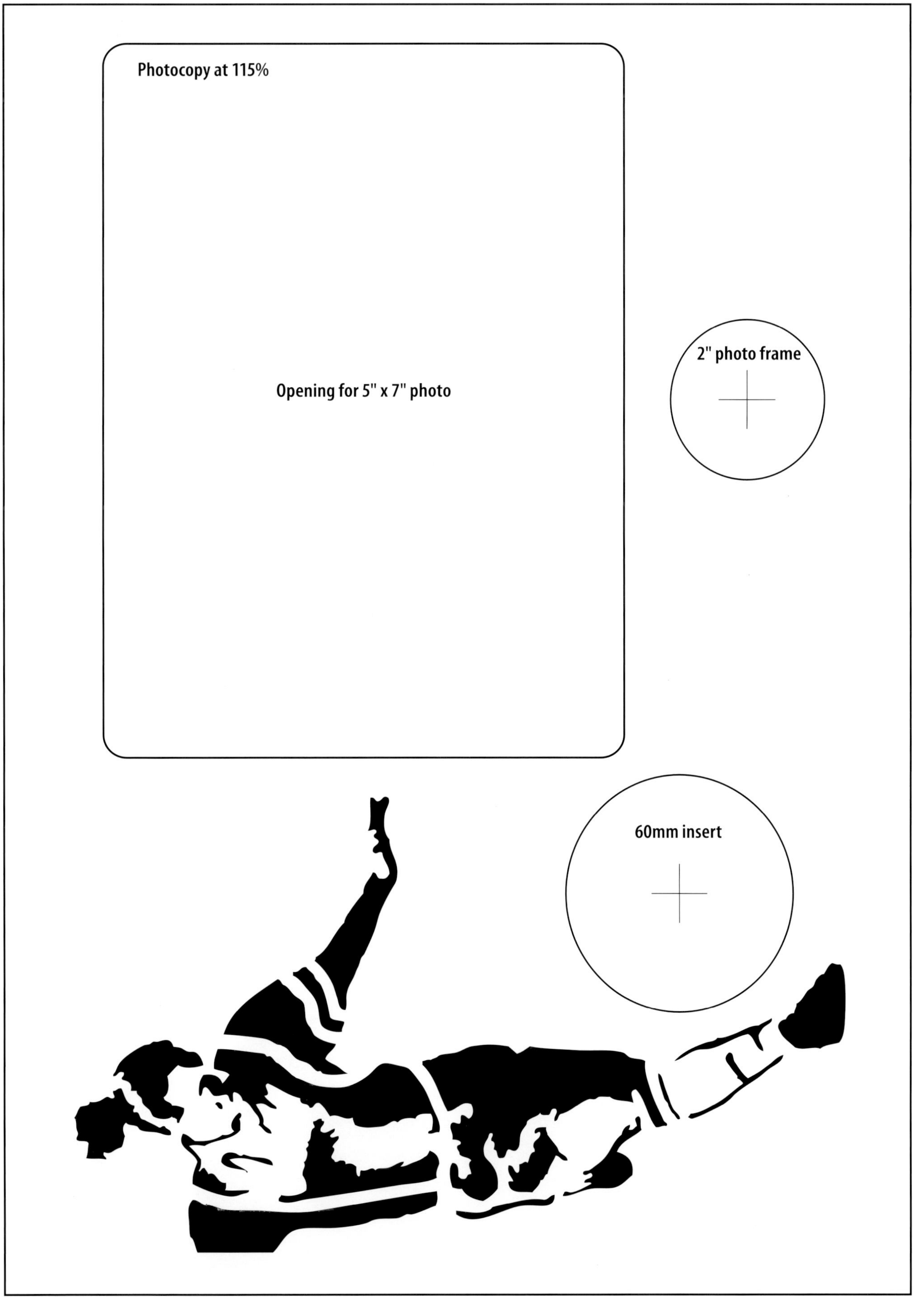

Photocopy at 115%

2" photo frame

Opening for 5" x 7" photo

60mm insert

Violin
Clock

A simple, elegant instrumental tribute

By Sue Mey

I love music, all kinds of music. But to me, there is something special about the violin. It's a beautiful instrument with flowing lines, and I find the magical sound that emanates from it truly breathtaking.

Size the pattern to accomodate the clock insert of your choice. Add a base to display the project on a desk or attach a hanger to mount on a wall. You could even reduce the pattern to make an attractive pin.

Photocopy at 100%

© 2009 Scroll Saw Woodworking & Crafts

Intermediate Clocks

The clocks in this section are more advanced than the beginner clocks, but they're worth the extra effort to develop your skills. Many of them will introduce you to new woodworking techniques, if you're interested in giving those options a try. Again, all of the projects featured have the information you need to complete them. For some, that includes full step-by-step instructions; for others, all you'll need is the pattern, photo, and materials list.

Simple Shaker Clock,
by Dennis Simmons, page 74.

A Valentine's Day Gift

Make this clock for your special someone

By Gary Hawkes

Puzzle clocks are real favorites of mine. I've done various shapes, but I think this is one of my favorites. Especially around Valentine's Day, this puzzle clock seems so appropriate. The old Janis Joplin song lyric "have another little piece of my heart" takes on a different meaning, doesn't it?

Step 1: Adhere the patterns. Glue the patterns to the stock using temporary bond spray adhesive.

Step 2: Drill the hole for the clock. Use the 1⅜" Forstner bit. The hole should be ¼" deep.

Step 3: Cut out the puzzle pieces. Use a #2 skip-tooth blade. The smaller the blade, the fewer gaps you'll have. Fewer gaps mean a tighter fit. I cut the bottom of the bottom puzzle piece at a 10-degree angle so that the clock will lean back just a tad.

Step 4: Sand. Using the 220-grit paper, round off the front facing edges of all pieces.

KEEPING IT TOGETHER   TIP

You're going to want to move the puzzle at some point. I've found that wrapping the puzzle in clear plastic wrap works the best.

Step 5: Stain the wood. I used Minwax Early American stain for the darker pieces. The lighter pieces are stained with a 50-50 mix of the Early American stain and paint thinner.

Step 6: Mount the clock. Next, mount the bottom puzzle piece and the hardboard backing to the base using wood glue.

Step 7: Assemble the puzzle.

Location of puzzle
and backing

Base
¾" stock

Photocopy at 100%

Materials & Tools

Materials:
- 1" x 12" x 8" clear poplar
  (or wood of choice) for the puzzle
- 1" x 5" x 5" clear poplar for the base
- 2" (50mm) clock inserts that fit in a
  1⅜"-diameter hole
- Temporary bond spray adhesive
- Minwax Early American Stain
  (or stain of your choice)
- Paint thinner
- 1⅜" x 12" x 8" hardboard
- Sandpaper, 220 grit
- Wood glue
- Varathane satin finish

Tools:
- Drill
- 1⅜" diameter Forstner bit
- #2 skip tooth blade

STAINING THE PIECES TIP

*Go to your cupboard and get one of those
old butter or margarine tubs for each of the
batches of stain you want. You'll also want
to get some rags for wiping off the excess
stain. For the dark pieces, just pour the
stain right in to the tub. If you want lighter
pieces, make a 50-50 mix of stain and
paint thinner. Stir until blended. Dip each
piece into the appropriate tub, remove
and wipe off the excess stain. Place on
newspaper to dry.*

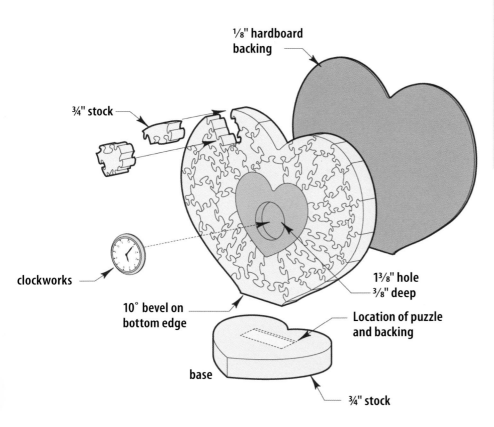

⅛" hardboard
backing

¾" stock

clockworks

10° bevel on
bottom edge

base

¾" stock

1⅜" hole
⅜" deep

Location of puzzle
and backing

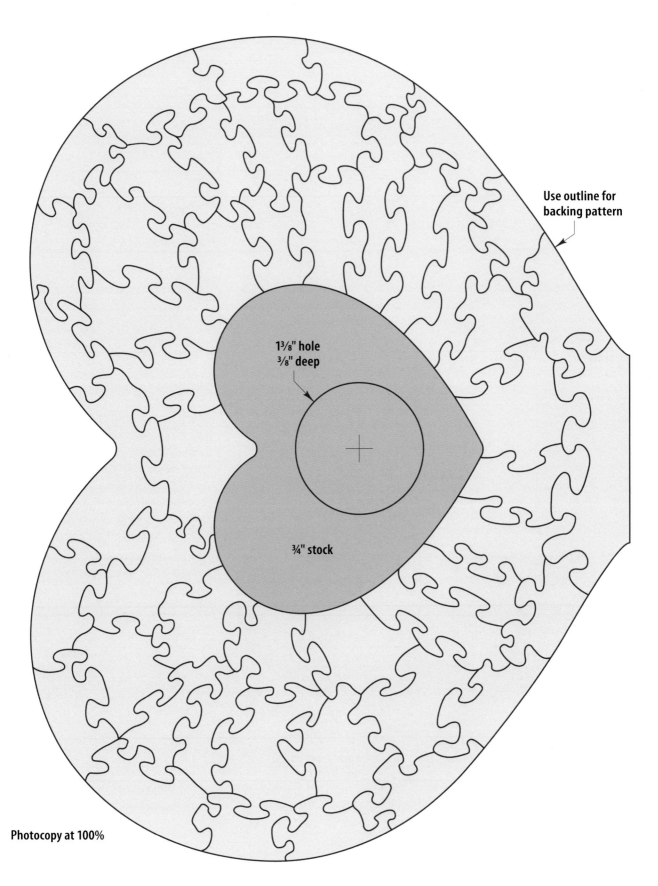

Use outline for
backing pattern

1³⁄₈" hole
³⁄₈" deep

¾" stock

Photocopy at 100%

Oval Wall Clock

Scroll this vintage project

By John A. Nelson

This pattern looks great displayed on its own or paired with a matching wall mirror. An oval clock completes the vintage look, but you could also use a round insert. I recommend ½" thick stock for this project. Use a nice hardwood with pretty grain such as maple, cherry, or walnut.

Materials & Tools

Materials:
- ½" x 11" x 17" maple, cherry, walnut, or wood of choice
- Masking tape
- Spray adhesive
- Sandpaper, assorted grits
- Danish oil, tung oil, or finish of choice
- Lint-free cloth
- Wood glue
- Hanger for wall mounting (optional)
- Clock insert of choice

Tools:
- #5 reverse-tooth blades or blades of choice
- Drill or drill press with bits to match size of clock insert and sizes of blades
- Sander of choice or sanding block
- Paintbrush for applying finish

2³/₈" diam.

Photocopy at 100%

Puzzle Clocks

This pair of poplar puzzle clocks is sure to bring hours of fun to the whole family.
By Gary Hawkes

The puzzle-clock idea was conceived about a year ago. When I first started scrolling, I really enjoyed making miniature clocks. Then, I started scrolling puzzles of all different shapes and sizes. One day I thought, "Let's combine the two." So I did, and the puzzle-clock concept was born. There are two to choose from here, each with slightly different designs and dimensions.

A #2 skip-tooth blade was used to make this project. This size blade is very thin and leaves fewer gaps. As the pieces are scrolled, put the puzzle together off to the side: This helps keep things in order and helps you check the fit.

I rounded off the front facing edges of each piece, which makes it easier to put together. Round off the edges on the base, too. The insert mounting holes are bored to a depth of ¼".

I used Minwax Early American stain on the darker pieces, but any dark stain will do. I thinned the stain with paint thinner by 50% for the lighter pieces. Carefully spread the pieces out on newspaper when finishing.

These puzzling puzzle clocks are the original creation of scroller Gary Hawkes. The pieces were fashioned from ¾" thick poplar and finished with alternating dark and light stains.

Materials:

- ¾" x 1' x 6" poplar (small clock & base)
- ¾" x 1' x 8" poplar (large clock & base)
- 1⁷⁄₁₆" (36mm) insert (small clock)
- 2" (50mm) insert (large clock)
- Dark stain of choice
- Paint thinner
- Plexiglas sheet, ¹⁄₁₆"
  or suitable ¹⁄₁₆" backing board
- #4 round head, ½" wood screws,
  two each
- Spray adhesive
- 220-grit sandpaper
- Transparent tape
- Wood glue
- Varathane or suitable
  clear spray finish

Tools:

- Hobby knife
- ¹⁄₁₆"-diameter drill bit
- 1⅜" Forstner bit (small insert)
- 1¹³⁄₁₆" Forstner bit (large insert)
- #2 skip-tooth blade

Home base: The bases of these clocks were shaped in classic puzzle piece form. Glue the bottom piece of the face of the clock to the base. The backing board is attached to the base via two round head ½" wood screws.

Anatomy of a puzzle clock: A ¹⁄₁₆" Plexiglas backing board serves as the backbone of this curious puzzle clock. The backer was scrolled with a #2 skip-tooth blade. This clock features a 2" movement housed in a 1¹³⁄₁₆" hole, which is ¼" deep.

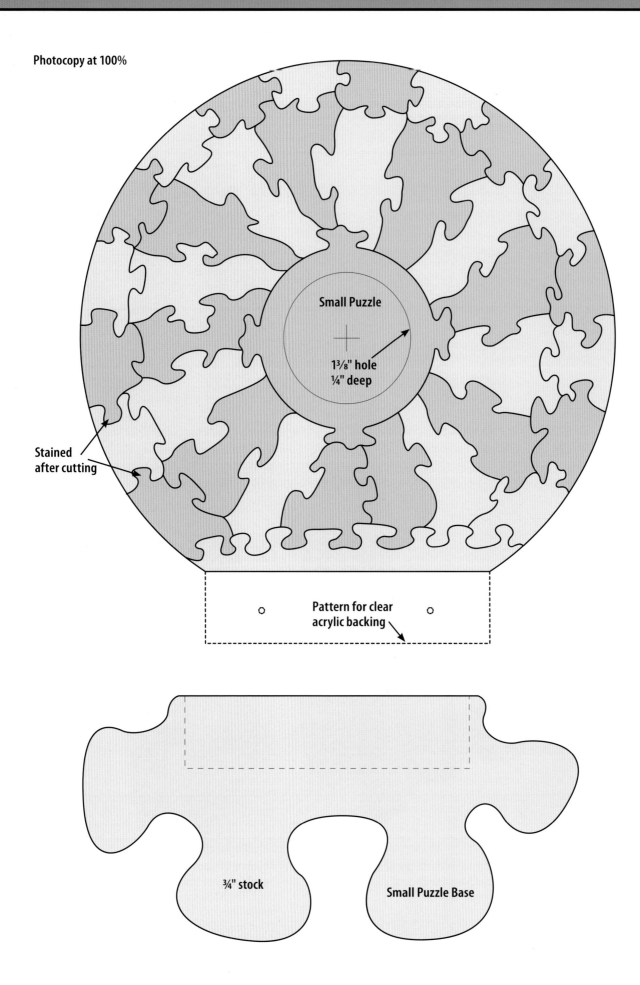

Small Puzzle

1³⁄₈" hole
¼" deep

Stained
after cutting

Pattern for clear
acrylic backing

¾" stock

Small Puzzle Base

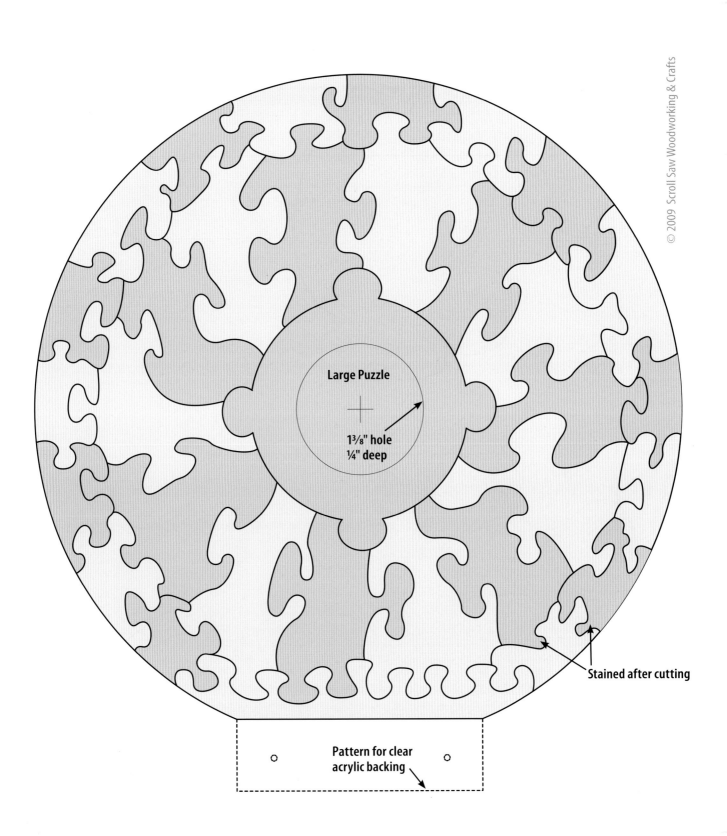

Large Puzzle

1³⁄₈" hole
¼" deep

Stained after cutting

Pattern for clear
acrylic backing

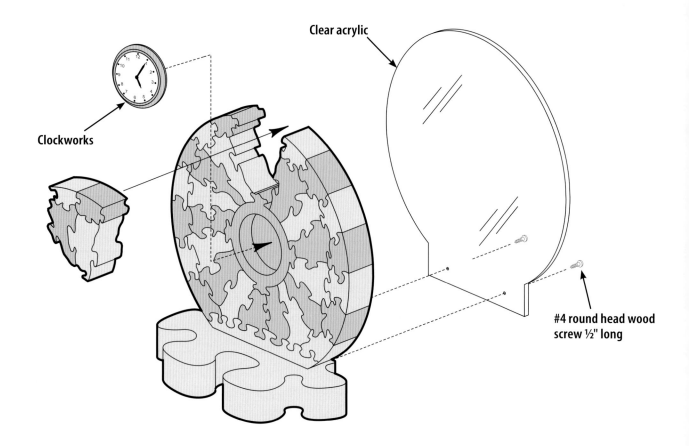

Clockworks

Clear acrylic

#4 round head wood screw ½" long

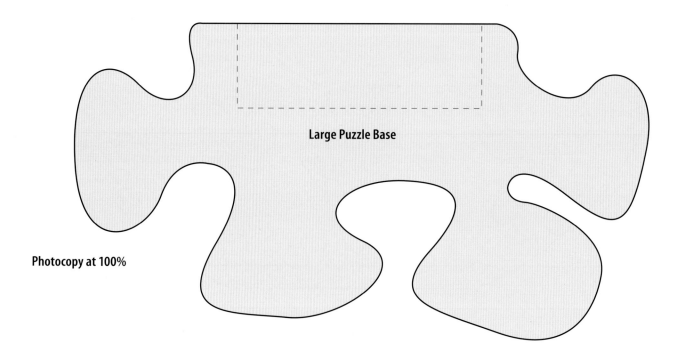

Large Puzzle Base

Photocopy at 100%

© 2009 Scroll Saw Woodworking & Crafts

Patriotic Clock

Practice your Plexiglas cutting skills

By Steve Greytak

The sharp points of the stars and the smooth curves of the stripes highlight this fun project. Scrolled from red, white, and blue Plexiglas, the Patriotic Clock gives you lots of practice with these somewhat difficult cuts, and when you're finished, you'll have a unique timepiece that shows off your American pride.

Step 1: Attach the pattern and cut the stars. Use rubber cement to attach the pattern for piece 1 to solid blue Plexiglas. (Because Plexiglas comes with a paper backing on it, I've found that rubber cement works very well.) Drill the blade entry holes with the ⅛" bit. Cut out the stars and the outer shape with the #3 blade (or blade of your choice).

Step 2: Cut the red stripes. Again, using rubber cement, attach the patterns for pieces 2, 3, 4, 5, and 6 to solid red Plexiglas. Cut all pieces per the pattern.

Step 3: Cut the white stripes. Using rubber cement one more time, attach the pattern for piece 7 to solid white Plexiglas. Cut the outer edge to shape. Remove the paper backing.

Step 4: Sand and glue. After lightly sanding the surfaces that will be glued, use cyanoacrylate (CA) glue or another super strength adhesive to attach pieces 1 and 2 to 7. Spread the glue on the back surfaces of pieces 1 and 2. Use glue sparingly and keep it away from the edges. Once the pieces are in place, clamp them together until the glue dries, usually between 10 and 20 seconds.

Step 5: Finish assembly. Attach pieces 3, 4, 5, and 6 to 7 with equal spacing between each part. Again, lightly sand the back surfaces. Apply a little glue to the back surfaces of pieces 3 through and including 6, then clamp until the glue sets up.

CUTTING PLEXIGLAS   TIP

The key to successfully cutting Plexiglas is to reduce heat buildup that causes the plastic to melt. Two things help reduce heat. The first is simply running your saw at a slower-than-usual speed. I run mine somewhere in the neighborhood of 850 strokes per minute; because each saw is a little different, your best bet is to experiment. The second is to cover the piece with duct tape in addition to the paper backing that is already attached to the Plexiglas when you buy it. The backing plus the tape keep the debris out of the kerf as you cut, thus reducing heat buildup.

Step 6: **Smooth the edges.** Sand the outer edge of piece 7 to match the edges of 1 and 2.

Step 7: **Drill.** With a 1⅜" Forstner bit, bore a 1⅜" hole in the centers of pieces 6 and 7.

Step 8: **Install the clock.** Insert 1⁷⁄₁₆" clock.

Step 9: **Display the project.** Display the finished clock on a plate stand. Or, if you'd like to hang the clock, attach a sawtooth hanger or other type of hook to the back using the CA glue or super strength adhesive.

Photocopy at 100%

USING A FORSTNER BIT ON PLEXIGLAS **TIP**

Boring holes in this plastic material can be a little tricky. It's best to go slowly and back out the bit frequently so the Plexiglas won't melt and cause problems with further cutting. At times, I saw the insert hole a little under 1⅜", then use a 1" drum sander to make a nice, snug fit.

GLUING PLEXIGLAS **TIP**

For best results, keep the glue away from the edges. Also, use the glue sparingly. A little glue goes a long way.

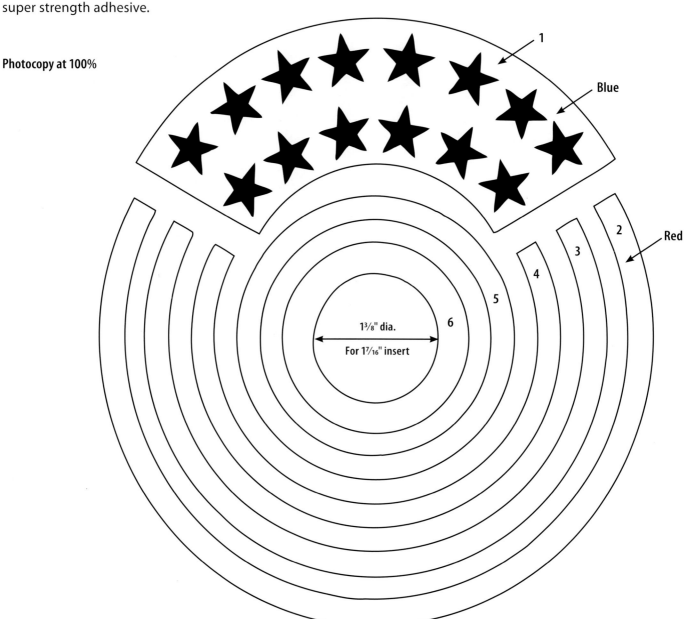

1
Blue
2
Red
3
4
5
6

1⅜" dia.
For 1⁷⁄₁₆" insert

GETTING SHARP POINTS **TIP**

To make the stars' sharp points, start at the blade entry hole and cut along one side to the tip. Once you're at the tip, stop pushing forward. Carefully pull the workpiece toward you, following the line you just cut. This is called "backing out." Once the blade returns to the entry hole, cut along the other side to the tip.

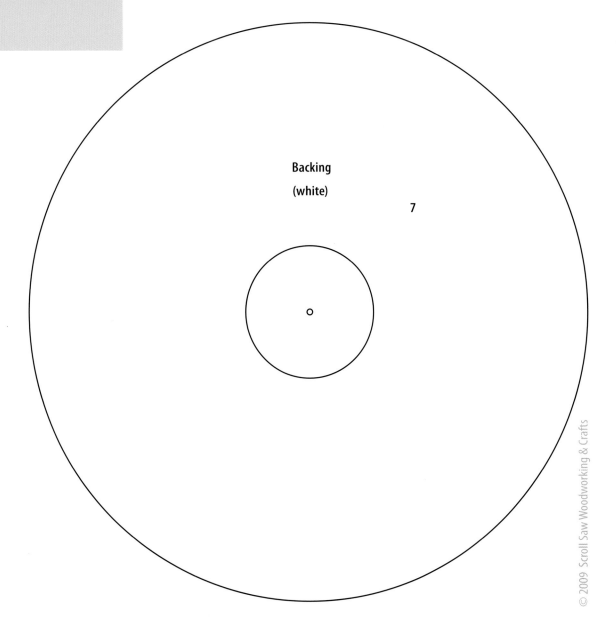

Backing

(white)

7

Miniature Grandfather Clock

This scaled-down version of a traditional grandfather clock is just as impressive as its full-size counterpart

By John Nelson
Cut by Ernest Lang

Materials & Tools

Materials:

Hardwood of choice:
- ⅜" x 3⅜" x 16" (1)
- 2 pieces ³⁄₁₆" x 2¼" x 3¼" (2)
- 2 pieces ³⁄₁₆" x 1¹⁄₁₆" x 2⅞" (3)
- 3 pieces ³⁄₁₆" x 2⁷⁄₁₆" x 3½" (4)
- ³⁄₁₆" x 2⁹⁄₁₆" x 3¹³⁄₁₆" (5)
- ³⁄₁₆" x 2⁹⁄₁₆" x 3¹³⁄₁₆" (6)
- 4 pieces ³⁄₁₆" x ⅞" x ⅞" (7)
- ³⁄₁₆" x 2¹³⁄₁₆" x 3¼" (8)
- 2 pieces ³⁄₁₆" x 2" x 7" (9)
- 2 pieces ³⁄₁₆" x 1⁵⁄₁₆" x 2⁷⁄₁₆" (10)
- ³⁄₁₆" x 2⅝" x 4³⁄₁₆" (11)
- ³⁄₁₆" x 2⁷⁄₁₆" x 7" (12)
- 2 pieces ³⁄₁₆" x 2⁷⁄₁₆" x 4⅞" (13)
- 2 pieces ³⁄₁₆" x 1¹¹⁄₁₆" x 3⅞" (14)
- ³⁄₁₆" x 1⁷⁄₁₆" x 3⁵⁄₁₆" (15)
- ³⁄₁₆" x 3⅜" x 5" (16)
- ³⁄₁₆" x 2⅝" x 4³⁄₁₆" (17)
- ³⁄₁₆" x 1½" x 5" (18)
- 2 pieces ⅜" diameter x ⁵⁄₁₆" long dowels (19)
- ³⁄₁₆" x ¾" x 1" (20)
- 2¼"-diameter mini clock insert
- Assorted grits of sandpaper
- Glue of choice
- Finish of choice

Tools:
- #5 and #1 reverse-tooth blades or blades of choice
- Drill with ⅜"- and ¹⁄₁₆"-diameter drill bits
- 2⅛"-diameter Forstner bit

For many woodworkers, a grandfather clock is the pinnacle of craftsmanship. But for most people, the details, joints, and sheer size of the project put it out of reach. This miniature version gives the average scroller an opportunity to create their own masterpiece.

The design is based on a copy of an antique pattern from Handicrafts Ltd., circa 1890. Several pieces of the clock are square or rectangular, with no frets or cutouts for joints. For best results, these pieces should be cut on a table saw. They can be cut on a scroll saw, but because the assembly of the clock requires that these pieces fit exactly, it is best to cut outside the lines, and sand up to them.

Step 1: Transfer the patterns to the work pieces. Cut the pieces to the dimensions listed in the Materials & Tools list. Since the material for most of the pieces is only ³⁄₁₆"-thick, it is easy to stack cut the blanks you need more than one piece of.

Step 2: Drill the holes for the project. Use a 1¹⁵⁄₁₆"-diameter Forstner bit for the clock face. Drill the two ⅜"-diameter holes where indicated on piece #18. Use a ¹⁄₁₆"-diameter bit to drill blade entry holes for the fretwork.

Step 3: Cut out the pieces. Use a #1 reverse-tooth blade for the fretwork. Use a #5 reverse-tooth blade to cut the perimeter of the pieces.

Step 4: Sand the pieces with 220-grit sandpaper. Double check to ensure the cutouts are square; otherwise you may have trouble assembling the clock.

Step 5: Dry assemble the clock. Start with piece #1 and add the other pieces to it in numerical order. This not only tests the fit of the pieces, but also lets you practice putting it together without worrying about getting glue on all the pieces. You can temporarily hold the pieces together with blue painter's tape. Disassemble the pieces after making any adjustments.

Step 6: Glue and clamp the pieces together. Again, start with piece #1 and add the pieces in numerical order. Remove any glue squeeze-out with a damp rag. Test cutter Ernie Lang used cyanoacrylate (CA) glue for assembly.

Step 7: Apply a spray lacquer finish. Ernie said the spray lacquer is easier to apply, and actually hides any discoloration caused by the CA glue.

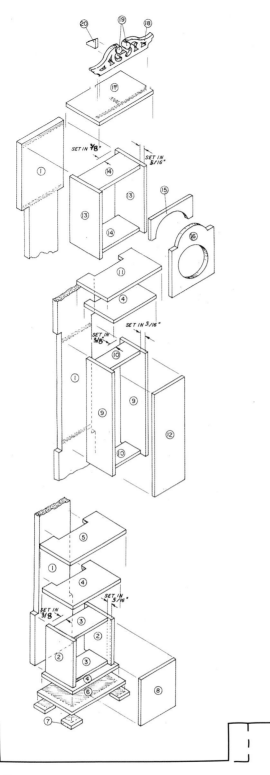

4 Make 2 - as shown
Make 1 - dashed lines

Photocopy at 100%

Use a 2¼" dia. insert

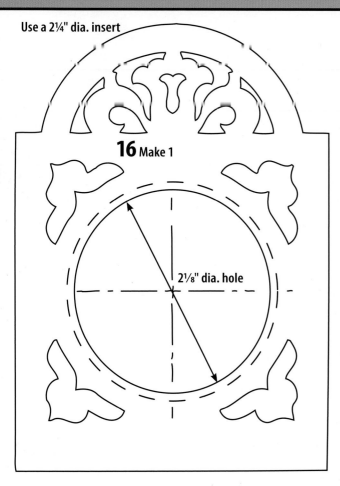

16 Make 1

2⅛" dia. hole

12 Make 1

⅜" dia.

19 Make 2

5/16"

⅜" dia. hole – 2 places

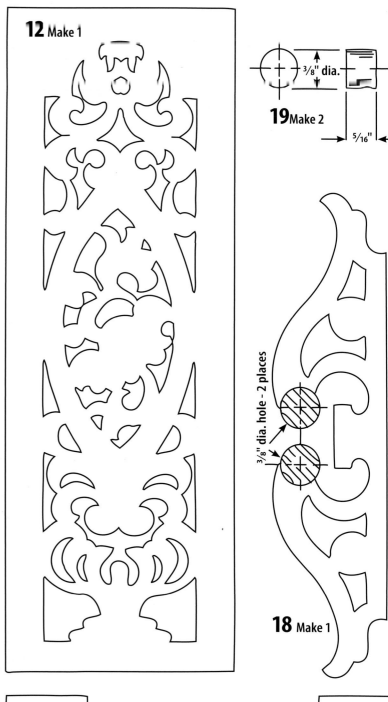

18 Make 1

8 Make 1

11 Make 1

Photocopy at 100%

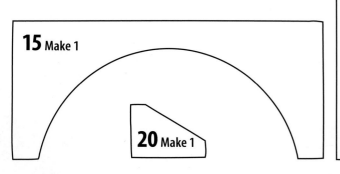

15 Make 1

20 Make 1

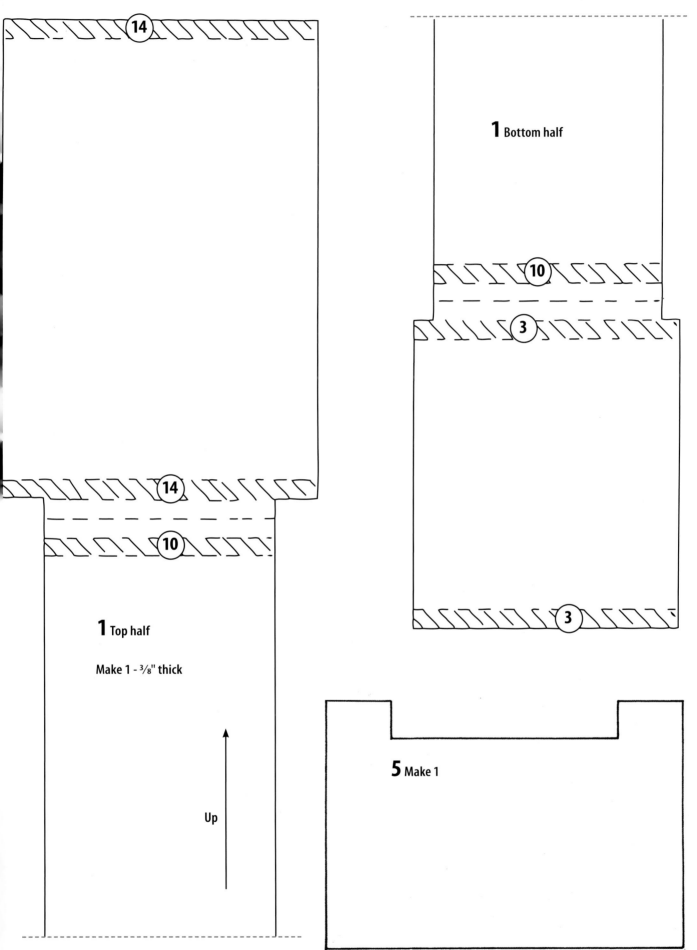

14

1 Bottom half

10

3

14

10

1 Top half

Make 1 - ³/₈" thick

Up

3

5 Make 1

Feline fans will purr when presented with this three-dimensional cat wall clock.

Cat Lover's Clock

Relief cutting gives this clock a 3-D look

By John A. Nelson

Here is a new slant on an old scroll saw technique: relief cutting. In this project we are going to use relief cutting to give a three-dimensional effect to a simple scroll saw pattern, a cat.

For the most part, relief cutting is just like regular scrolling, with one main difference: in relief cutting you tilt your table 2° to 2½° and cut in only one direction to make the pieces project from the face of the board. Cutting the other direction recesses the pieces.

There is no substitute for test cutting to determine the proper table angle and cutting direction. Trace a quarter-sized oval on scrap wood, tilt your table down 2°, and use the same blade you will for the project to cut around the oval. Note whether you are cutting clockwise or counterclockwise.

You will get the same result by tilting the opposite side of your table down and cutting in the same direction. You will get the reverse result by leaving the table tilted in the same direction and cutting in the opposite direction. Increase the tilt to 2½° and cut another practice oval. Experiment until you get a piece that projects forward about ³⁄₁₆" from the face. Once you get the right combination, write it on your pattern and draw a directional arrow for each piece to keep you on track while cutting.

RELIEF CUTTING CONTROLS   TIP

Relief cutting techniques are controlled by three facts:
• Blade thickness
• Degree of table slant (usually to the left)
• Direction of cut (clockwise or counterclockwise.)

If any of the three are changed, the results will be different, so keep these variables constant throughout your project.

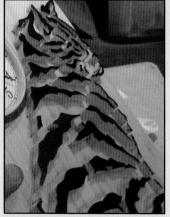

USING EXISTING PATTERNS   TIP

The relief cutting techniques for projecting or recessing may work well with other patterns you already have. Have fun experimenting!

Preparing to Cut

1 **Prepare the wood.** Sand the top and bottom surfaces after cutting the wood to size. Sand all the edges using medium then fine sandpaper. I use a palm sander, but sandpaper wrapped around a block of wood would do. Then, wipe the wood to remove all the sanding dust.

2 **Seal the wood.** Apply two or three coats of a clear, satin finish of your choice. Make sure to finish the front, back, and edges.

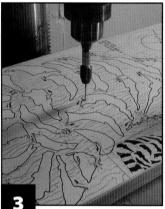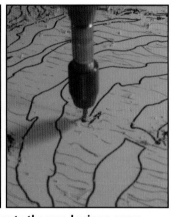

3 **Attach the marked pattern to the wood using a spray adhesive.** Carefully drill all blade entry holes using a 1/32"-diameter bit in the drill press. It is important that you drill the holes at the black dots as shown on the pattern.

Cutting the Design

4 **Set the tilt of your table** according to the specifications you wrote on the pattern and carefully make all cuts in the same direction, following the arrows. Do not stop and reverse direction; continue around back to the starter hole, following the arrow on the pattern. As you make each cut, lock the piece in place by pushing through to the front until snug, so you will not lose it.

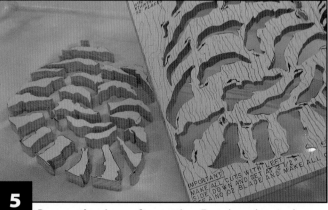

5 **Remove the pieces after cutting.** Try to keep them in about the same location and position as they are on the pattern. You can number them to make replacing them easier. Then, turn the piece over and sand the back to remove any burrs.

6 **Remove the pattern and drill.** Carefully remove the pattern by spraying it with paint thinner. Then, locate and drill the hole for the clock insert. Make sure to match the size of the hole to the insert you have chosen.

Finishing

7 **Attach the hanger and paint.** Before installing the clock insert, attach the hanger to the center of the back of the work piece. Paint the face surface of each piece of the cutouts using a piece of cloth—dab a little black acrylic artist paint onto the cloth. Using your index finger, apply the paint to the face surface of each piece. Take care not to get any paint on the edges—only paint the faces of the pieces. After the paint dries, apply a coat of clear matte polyurethane finish on the face of the pieces that are painted black, making sure not to let it get on the edges of the pieces.

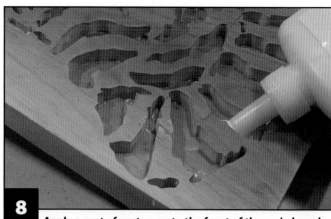

8 **Apply a coat of paste wax to the front of the main board.** Then, add the pieces of the cat and lock each piece in place about ³⁄₁₆" above the surface. Double check to make sure all the pieces stick out about ³⁄₁₆" and that they are all on the same plane. Turn over and add glue inside each opening. Let the glue dry a little bit.

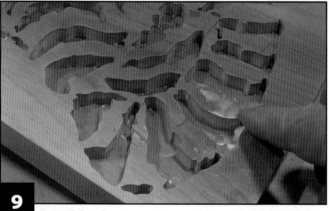

9 **Spread the glue.** Smooth glue out with your index finger before it dries totally.

10 **Install the clock.** To give the clock a "finished look," glue a piece of cardboard to the back. Add a battery to the clock insert and attach it to the board. It should fit tightly in the hole.

Materials & Tools

Materials:
- Soft, knot-free wood ¾" thick
- 2³⁄₈"-diameter clock insert (or insert of your choice)
- Satin clear spray or brush-on finish
- Black artist acrylic paint
- Clear matte polyurethane finish
- Light stain (optional)
- Wood glue
- Cardboard

Tools:
- #2 blade
- Sandpaper, medium through fine grits
- Forstner bit to fit the clock insert you choose
- Drill press
- ¹⁄₃₂"-diameter drill bit
- Palm sander (optional) or sanding block

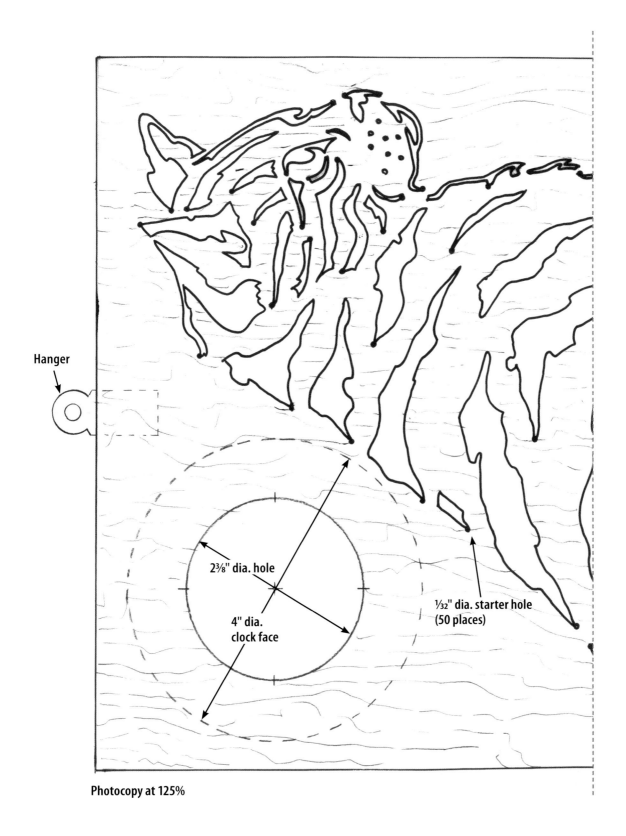

Hanger

2³⁄₈" dia. hole

4" dia.
clock face

¹⁄₃₂" dia. starter hole
(50 places)

Photocopy at 125%

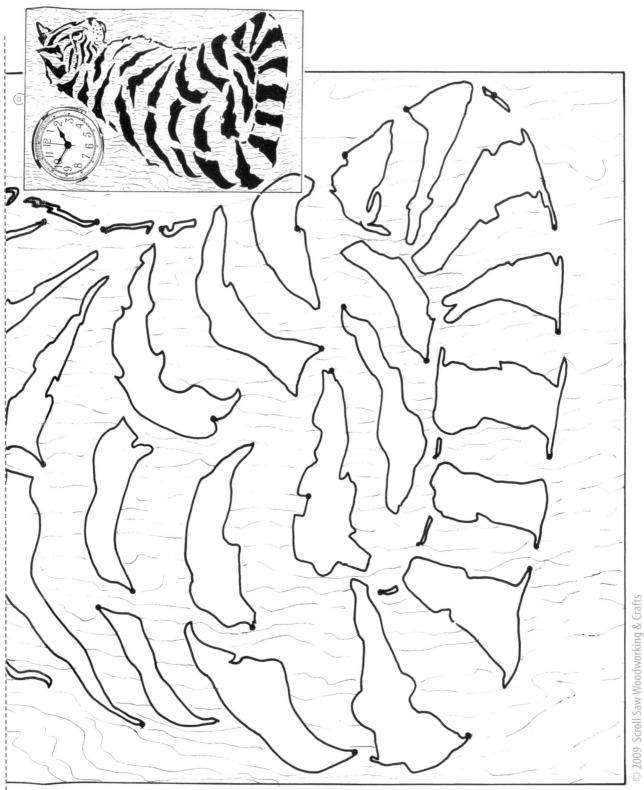

Photocopy at 125%

Keep the cutting conditions constant, using a no. 2 blade and following the specifications and arrows you put on the pattern.

Woven Box Clocks

A keepsake to make and give

By John A. Nelson

If you're searching for a special gift or for the right presentation of that special gift, a heart-shaped box may be just the thing. Perfect for jewelry or other small keepsakes, give a handmade box that he or she will treasure.

I got the idea for this box when I discovered heart-shaped hinges from National Artcraft Co. They were originally used for ceramic projects, but I found they make wonderful hinges for these wooden boxes.

To help make assembly very easy and exact, two ⅛"-diameter dowel guides (F) are used. My good friend Bill Guimond made the boxes pictured, and his wife, Colette Guimond, painted the lids. Bill does not believe in stack cutting, but he has the uncanny ability to cut out ten individual pieces so exact that, if you stack them, they line up perfectly. I stack cut to save time and to ensure all the pieces are exactly the same.

Materials & Tools

Materials:

- 1 piece, ⅛" contrasting hardwood of choice with straight grain for Base A
- 4 pieces, ¼" hardwood of choice with straight grain for Weave B
- 3 pieces, ¼" hardwood of choice with straight grain for Weave C
- 1 piece, ⅛" hardwood of choice with straight grain for Top Lip D
- 1 piece, ½" contrasting hardwood of choice with straight grain for Lid E
- 2, ⅛"-diameter dowels (F)
- Large heart-shaped hinge
- Sandpaper, fine or extra fine grit
- 1⁷⁄₁₆"(36mm)-diameter clock insert (optional)
- Temporary bond spray adhesive
- Epoxy
- Yellow woodworker's glue
- ½"-diameter felt pads

Tools:

- #2 or #2/0 blade
- Router with bit of choice and follower
- Drill with ⅛"-diameter bit, and 1⅜" Forstner bit

Step 1: Cut and sand the wood. Cut the wood about ¼" over the size of the pattern. Sand the top and bottom surfaces with fine-grit sandpaper to remove any burrs.

Step 2: Affix the patterns. Make copies of the patterns and adhere them to the wood with temporary bond spray adhesive. Note: Some pieces require one of each, while others require more.

Step 3: Drill ⅛"-diameter holes as shown. If you stack cut, be sure to stack the pieces first, then drill through all the pieces at the same time. If you don't have a drill press, check that you're drilling straight up and down.

Step 4: Cut out all pieces. Use a #2 or #2/0 blade. Sand the top and bottom surfaces with fine-grit sandpaper to remove any burrs. Fit Top Lip D and Lid E to the hinge. Make sure the fit is snug.

Step 5: Stack and glue the parts. Using two ⅛"-diameter dowel guides (F) and yellow woodworker's glue, stack and glue all of the pieces together except Top Lip D, the hinge, and Lid E. (See the Assembly Drawing for the order of assembly.)

Step 6: Fit Lid E to the hinge. Make sure the fit is snug, then rout Lid E as shown. Using a Forstner bit, drill a 1⅜"-diameter hole ¼" deep for the clock insert (optional).

Step 7: Install the hinge. Glue Top Lip D and Lid E to the hinge using epoxy.

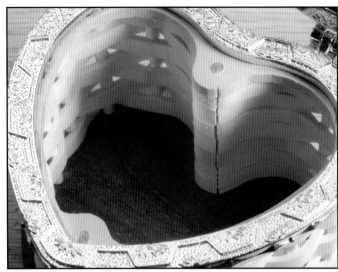

Step 8: Glue the top lid. Using yellow woodworker's glue, glue the Top Lip/hinge/Lid combination to the rest of the basket.

Step 9: Sand and finish. Lightly sand with extra-fine-grit sandpaper and finish as desired.

CHECKING FOR A 90° CUTTING ANGLE TIP

When stack cutting, make sure your blade is cutting straight up and down. To test this, take a piece of scrap wood and make a short cut in it. Pull the wood back from the blade. Place the wood behind the blade, turning the piece so the cut is facing the back of the blade. Slide the wood across the table so the blade goes into the cut. If the blade fits smoothly, your blade is square to the table. If the blade doesn't, you'll need to adjust the table until the fit is smooth.

WHAT'S A FOLLOWER ? TIP

Sometimes called a follower bit, a follower is a ball bearing roller mounted on the bottom of the shaft as a guide. This roller allows the bit to follow an edge with relative ease, eliminating the need for an elaborate fence guide.

Heart-shaped Keepsake Box

Assembly Drawing

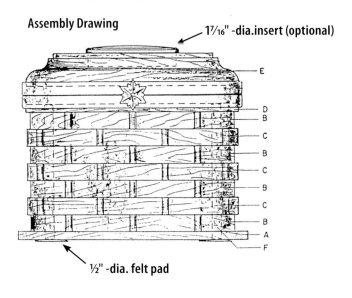

1⁷⁄₁₆"-dia. insert (optional)

E
D
B
C
B
C
B
C
B
A
F

½"-dia. felt pad

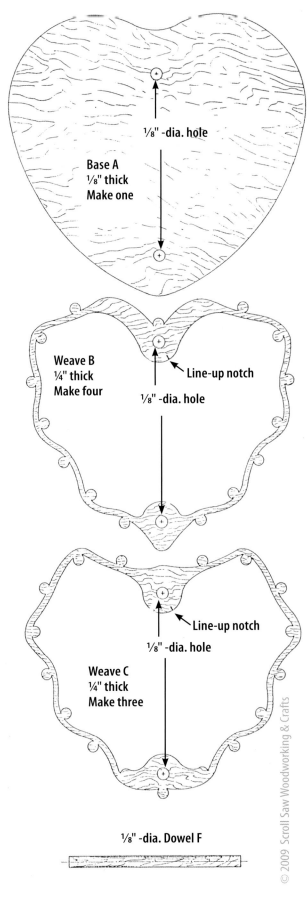

⅛"-dia. hole

Base A
⅛" thick
Make one

Weave B
¼" thick
Make four

Line-up notch

⅛"-dia. hole

Weave C
¼" thick
Make three

Line-up notch

⅛"-dia. hole

⅛"-dia. Dowel F

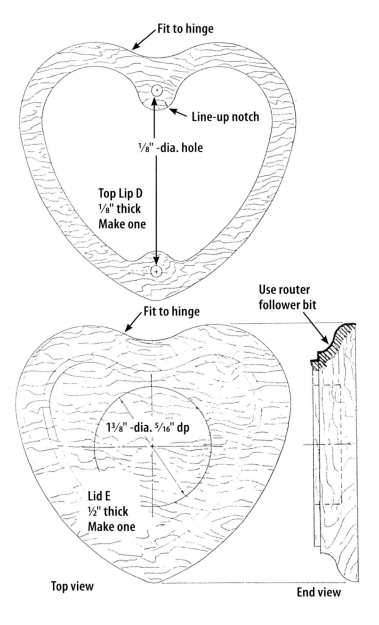

Fit to hinge

Line-up notch

⅛"-dia. hole

Top Lip D
⅛" thick
Make one

Fit to hinge

Use router
follower bit

1³⁄₈"-dia. ⁵⁄₁₆" dp

Lid E
½" thick
Make one

Top view

End view

© 2009 Scroll Saw Woodworking & Crafts

Round Keepsake Box

Photocopy at 110%

Assembly Drawing

1⁷/₁₆" -dia. insert (optional)

E
D
B
C
B
C
B
C
B
A
F

½" -dia. felt pad

Fit to hinge

¹/₈" -dia. hole

Top Lip D
¹/₈" thick
Make one

Line-up notch

Fit to hinge

Use router
follower bit

1³/₈" -dia. ⁵/₁₆ dp

Lid E
½" thick
Make one

Top view

End view

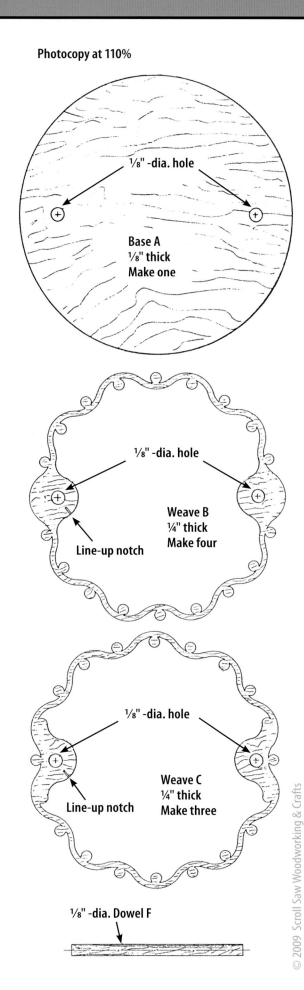

¹/₈" -dia. hole

Base A
¹/₈" thick
Make one

¹/₈" -dia. hole

Weave B
¼" thick
Make four

Line-up notch

¹/₈" -dia. hole

Weave C
¼" thick
Make three

Line-up notch

¹/₈" -dia. Dowel F

Lizard Desk Clock

Create this beautiful antique design in hardwood

By John A. Nelson

This Lizard Desk Clock looks great cut from a hardwood such as maple or walnut. I recommend ½"- to ⅝"-thick stock. When I saw the original design in an antique pattern, I was reminded of the circle of life, and I thought it was a perfect design to turn into a desk clock. With a few modifications, the pattern would also make a nice trivet or suncatcher.

Materials & Tools

Materials:
- ½"–⅝" x 8½" x 8" maple, walnut, or wood of choice
- Masking tape
- Spray adhesive
- Sandpaper, assorted grits
- Danish oil, tung oil, or finish of choice
- Lint-free cloth
- Wood glue
- Clock insert of choice

Tools:
- #5 reverse-tooth blades or blades of choice
- Drill or drill press with bits to match size of clock insert and sizes of blades
- Sander of choice or sanding block
- Paintbrush for applying finish

1⅜" dia.

Photocopy at 140%

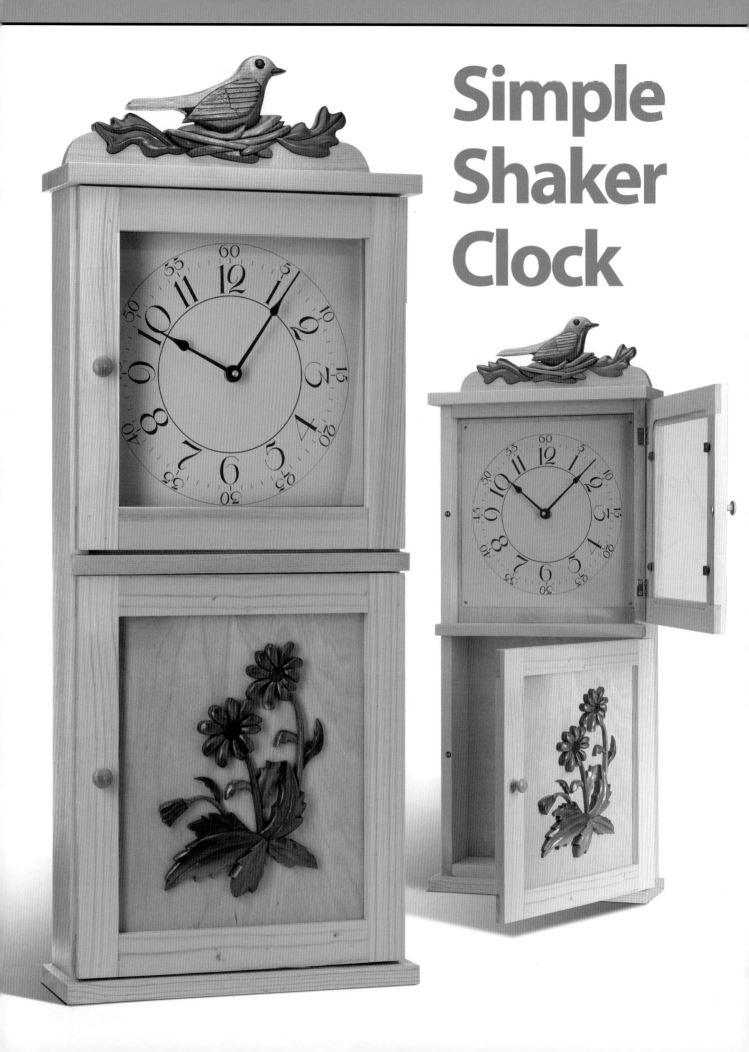

Simple Shaker Clock

Embellish this classic design with seasonal intarsia elements

By Dennis Simmons

Many scrollers create intarsia as stand-alone decorations, but with a bit of creativity, you can embellish a wide variety of projects with intarsia. The classic styling of this shaker clock makes it an appealing project to accent most décors. You can customize the clock with a wide variety of intarsia designs, or even use fretwork on the bottom door panel for a broader range of possibilities. The lower door design features a removable panel that allows you to create several designs that can be changed seasonally.

I designed the project to be made from standard-sized pine boards available at most retailers, so you do not need a table saw to rip the lumber to size. Cut the pieces to the dimensions listed in the materials list. Use the measured cutting guide for the center divider. The half-lap joints of the doors are cut on a scroll saw.

Exploded Drawing

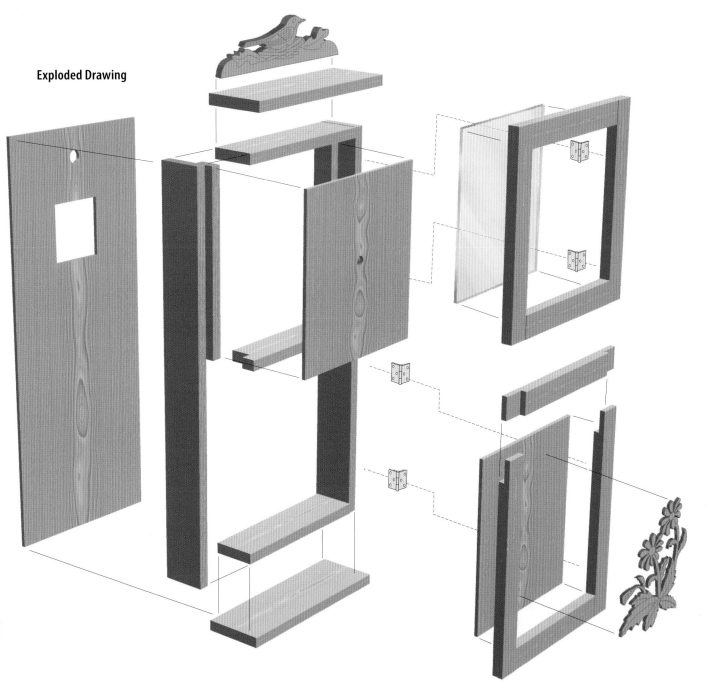

Making the Clock Case

1 **Dry fit the frame to ensure a correct fit.** Notice the support blocks highlighted in yellow. Drill the hanging hole and cut out the clock movement access hole using the measured drawing as a guide. Glue and nail the clock case pieces together. Do not attach the case top piece until the intarsia is complete.

2 **Cut half-lap joints for the door frames.** Use the measured drawing to mark the lap joints. Clamp the stock to a 2x4 wood block to help keep it square with the blade. Cut the notch with a thick-wood blade. Use the same technique to cut the joints on both ends of all eight door frame parts.

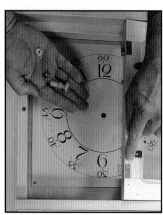

3 **Assemble the door frames.** Use wood glue and two small brad nails or screws to complete each lap joint. It is important to keep all of the corners square. The straighter your cuts, the easier it is to keep the corners square. Attach the glass and panel to the frames using your method of choice (see Mounting Door Panels, page 79).

4 **Finish assembling the case.** Drill the hole for the clock stem. Use the measured drawing as a guide. Mount the hinges. Check the dimensions of the hardware you are using for the wood knobs and magnetic catches. Drill corresponding holes on the doors and case frames.

Making the Intarsia Design

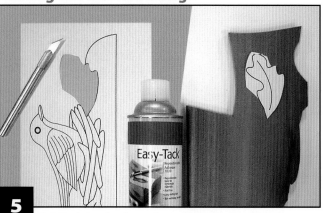

5 **Cut the intarsia pieces.** Cut each pattern piece from the main pattern. Position the pattern pieces on the wood. Pay special attention to the color and grain. Attach the patterns to the wood with spray adhesive. Cut the pieces with a #5 skip-tooth blade.

6 **Shape the intarsia pieces.** Secure the large pieces to a table with double-sided tape. Shape the pieces with carving tools and sanding tools. Use double-sided tape to attach the small pieces to scrap wood for sanding and shaping.

Assembling the Intarsia and Clock

7 **Assemble the intarsia.** Apply a coat of finish to the pieces. When dry, lay the pieces on wax paper, put a little cyanoacrylate (CA) glue on the contact points, and press the parts together for 15–30 seconds. Set everything aside for an hour. When the glue is completely dry, the piece can be picked up as one unit.

8 **Glue the flowers to the door panel.** Scuff the back of the intarsia with 80-grit sandpaper. Dry fit the intarsia and mark the location on the door panel with masking tape. Apply wood glue to the back of the intarsia with a small paint brush. Carefully position the intarsia on the panel and clamp in place until dry.

9 **Complete the bird and nest intarsia.** Use the same techniques explained above. All pieces are glued to a ⅛"-thick piece of plywood. Drill holes in the case top cap ⅜" from the back edge and 2" in from each end. Attach the intarsia to the top cap by inserting screws through the pre-drilled holes into the intarsia. Apply wood finish to the entire project and allow to dry.

10 **Finish assembling the clock.** Attach the clock face to the clock face backing using your method of choice. Install the clock mechanism according to the manufacturer's directions. Use wood glue to attach the clock face to the support blocks inside the upper case. Install the door hardware, panel and glass, and attach the doors to the clock case. Be sure to sign your work.

Materials & Tools

Materials:
- 2 pieces ¾" x 28" x 3" pine (case sides)
- 2 pieces ¾" x 11½" x 3" pine (case ends)
- 2 pieces ¾" x 13¾" x 4¼" pine (case top & bottom)
- ¼" x 28" x 12⅛" birch plywood (case back)
- 2 pieces ¾" x 12¼" x 1½" pine (support blocks)
- ¾" x 13" x 2½" pine (center divider)
- ¼" x 12¼" x 11½" birch plywood (clock face backing)
- 6 pieces ¾" x 12¾" x 1½" pine (short door frame pieces)
- 2 pieces ¾" x 14¼" x 1½" pine (long door frame pieces)
- ¼" x 11¾" x 10¼" birch plywood (lower door panel)
- ⅛" x 10¼" x 10¼" clear acrylic or glass (upper door panel)
- ¾" x 12" x 12" poplar or green wood of choice (intarsia)
- ¾" x 12" x 6" aromatic cedar or red wood of choice (intarsia)
- ¾" x 12" x 6" spruce or gray wood of choice (intarsia)
- ¾" x 6" x 6" western red cedar or brown wood of choice (intarsia)
- 2 shaker wood knobs
- 2 magnetic catches
- 4 door hinges
- 8 glass or mirror retainer clips
- Clock movement
- 11" x 11" clock face
- Temporary adhesive (to attach patterns)
- Wood finish of choice
- Carpet tape
- Cyanoacrylate (CA) glue
- Wood glue
- Scrap 2" x 4" (to clamp door frames)

Tools:
- Drill with ¹³⁄₃₂"-, ⅜"-, and ¹¹⁄₃₂"-diameter drill bits
- Clamping weights and foam packing
- #5 and thick-wood scroll saw blades or blades of choice
- Paintbrush (to apply glue to intarsia)
- Assorted clamps

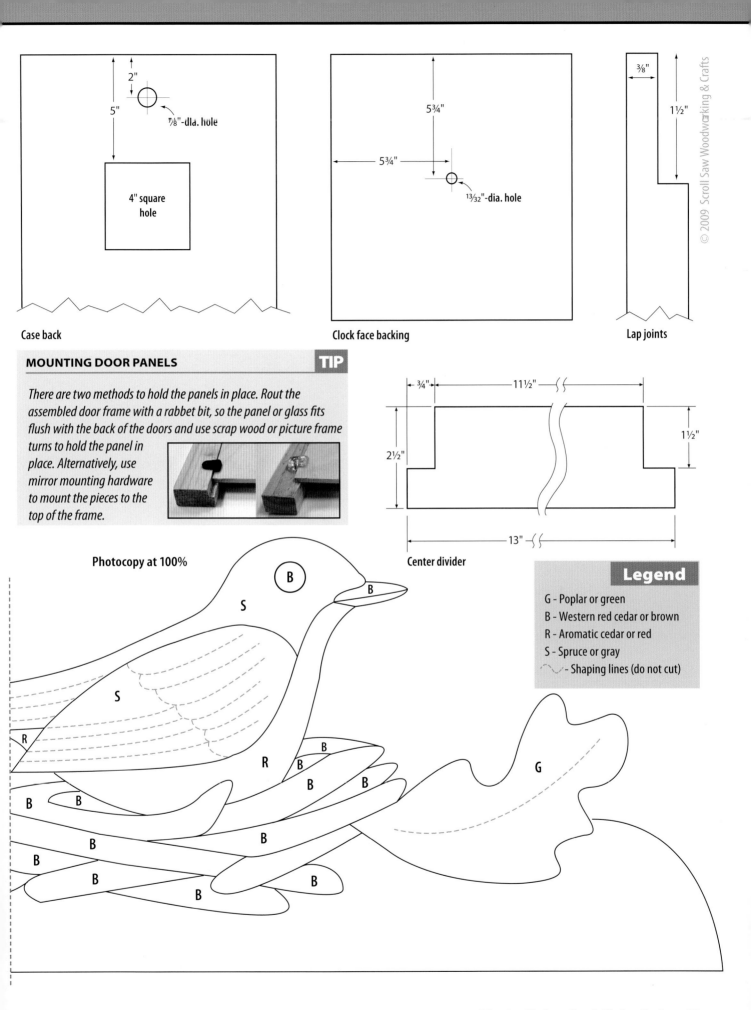

2"

5"

⅞"-dia. hole

4" square
hole

Case back

5¾"

5¾"

¹³⁄₃₂"-dia. hole

Clock face backing

3⁄8"

1½"

Lap joints

MOUNTING DOOR PANELS

TIP

There are two methods to hold the panels in place. Rout the assembled door frame with a rabbet bit, so the panel or glass fits flush with the back of the doors and use scrap wood or picture frame turns to hold the panel in place. Alternatively, use mirror mounting hardware to mount the pieces to the top of the frame.

¾"

11½"

2½"

1½"

13"

Center divider

Photocopy at 100%

B

B

S

S

R

R

B

B

B

B

B

B

B

B

B

B

B

G

Legend

G - Poplar or green
B - Western red cedar or brown
R - Aromatic cedar or red
S - Spruce or gray
〰️ - Shaping lines (do not cut)

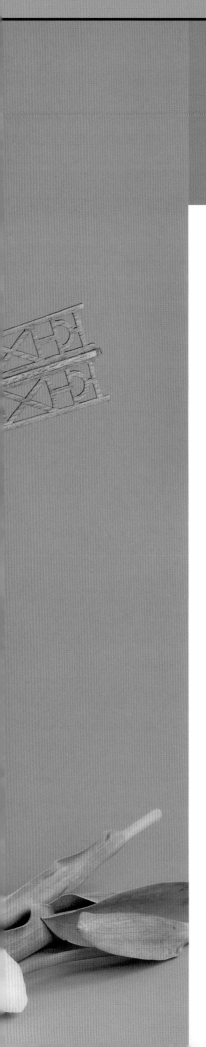

Master Clocks

In this section, advanced clock makers will find clocks that can sharpen their skills and inspire them in their own designs. The projects featured in this section can provide great ideas for gifts, commissions, and more.

Windmill Clock
by Pedro Lopez, page 112

Watchful Leopard Clock

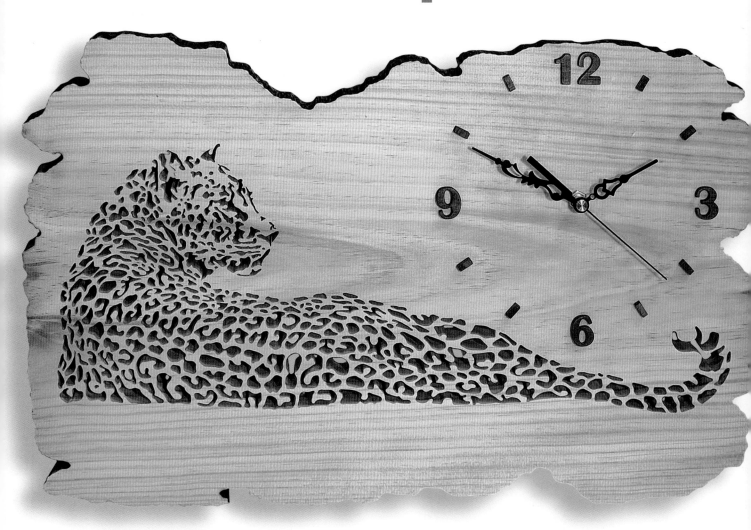

Use a woodburner to create the look of found wood

By Sue Mey

This striking leopard pattern, with nearly 400 frets, makes an attractive portrait on its own, but it is even more stunning when incorporated into a "found wood" wall clock. Scroll your own numerals for the clock face or simplify the project by adding a clock insert instead of the quartz movement.

Any light-colored hardwood is suitable. Simple cutting and burning techniques turn a standard blank into a natural-looking slab of found wood.

To get started, presand the wood using 150-grit and 320-grit sandpaper before applying the pattern. Use a palm sander. This reduces the hand sanding to be done later and the risk of breaking the fragile fretwork.

Prepare the Wood and Cut the Pattern

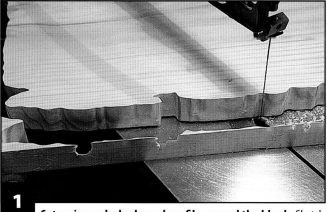

1 **Cut an irregularly shaped profile around the blank.** Sketch in the profile with a pencil, and cut along the lines with a #7 blade. Remember to leave room for the leopard and clock. After the leopard is cut, you can cut some extra curves if desired.

2 **Transfer the pattern to the blank.** Cover the surface of the wood with masking tape. Attach the pattern to the blank with temporary bond spray adhesive. Position the pattern toward the left side of the blank so you have room to add the clock.

3 **Drill the blade entry holes.** Use a 1/16"-diameter bit when possible. Switch to a 1/32"-diameter bit for the small openings. Use a backer board to prevent tear out. Scrape away any fuzz or splinters from the back with a utility knife held at a slight angle.

4 **Cut the frets.** Use a #7 blade for most of the cuts. Switch to a #2 and #2/0 blade for the progressively smaller openings. Slow your saw down, and use a zero-clearance table insert. Remove the pattern and masking tape. Reshape the outside profile if desired.

5 **Cut the numbers.** Use double-sided tape to attach two blanks together. Cut the numbers with a #2 blade. Stack cutting provides extra support, gives you more control with the thin material, and you have an extra if a piece breaks when sanding.

6 **Position the clock.** Draw a 6 5/16"-diameter circle in the upper right section. Drill a hole in the center of the circle to match the size of your clock stem. Trace the position of the movement on the back and recess the cavity with a router or carving tools.

Texture, Finish, and Assemble

7 **Add texture to the edges.** Use a woodburner with your tip of choice to create irregular impressions around the perimeter. Hand sand the front and back with 320-grit sandpaper. Switch to 500-grit sandpaper for a smooth finish. Use needle files to clean up the frets. Remove the sanding dust.

8 **Apply a finish.** Use a medium-sized artists' brush to apply deep-penetrating furniture wax liquid or Danish oil to the plaque. Apply walnut wood stain to the front and sides of the numbers. When dry, wipe all the surfaces with a dry, lint-free cloth to remove any residue.

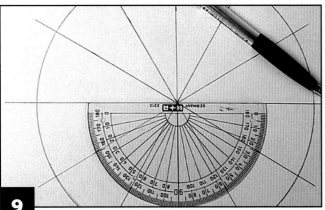

9 **Determine the clock layout.** Use a protractor to create a template for spacing the numerals and hash marks (representing the numbers not listed). Cut a hole in the center and align it with the clock stem hole. Transfer the position of the hash marks to the clock, using carbon paper and a stylus.

10 **Attach the numbers.** Use a toothpick to apply small beads of wood glue to the back of each hash mark and glue them in place. Then, arrange the numbers between the hash marks. Tweezers make it easy to position the tiny pieces. Use a toothpick to remove any glue squeeze-out.

11 **Apply a final finish.** Spray on several thin coats of clear varnish. Allow the varnish to dry thoroughly between coats and sand it lightly with 500-grit sandpaper. Attach a sawtooth hanger to the back. Install the clock movement according to the manufacturer's instructions.

Materials & Tools

Materials:
- 1" x 12" x 18½" light-colored hardwood of choice (clock)
- ⅛"-thick scraps of Baltic birch plywood (clock numbers)
- Masking tape
- Temporary bond spray adhesive
- Sandpaper, assorted grits
- Carbon paper
- Walnut wood stain
- Deep-penetrating furniture wax liquid or Danish oil
- Clear spray varnish
- Quartz movement and hands
- Sawtooth hanger

Tools:
- #2/0, #2, and #7 reverse, skip-tooth blades or blades of choice
- Drill press with ¹⁄₁₆"-, ¹⁄₃₂"- and ⁵⁄₁₆"-diameter bits (or appropriate bit for clock shaft)
- Palm sander
- Woodburning tool with tips of choice
- Carving tools or router
- Medium-sized artists' brush
- Lint-free cloth
- Stylus
- Compass
- Needle files
- Sharp pencil

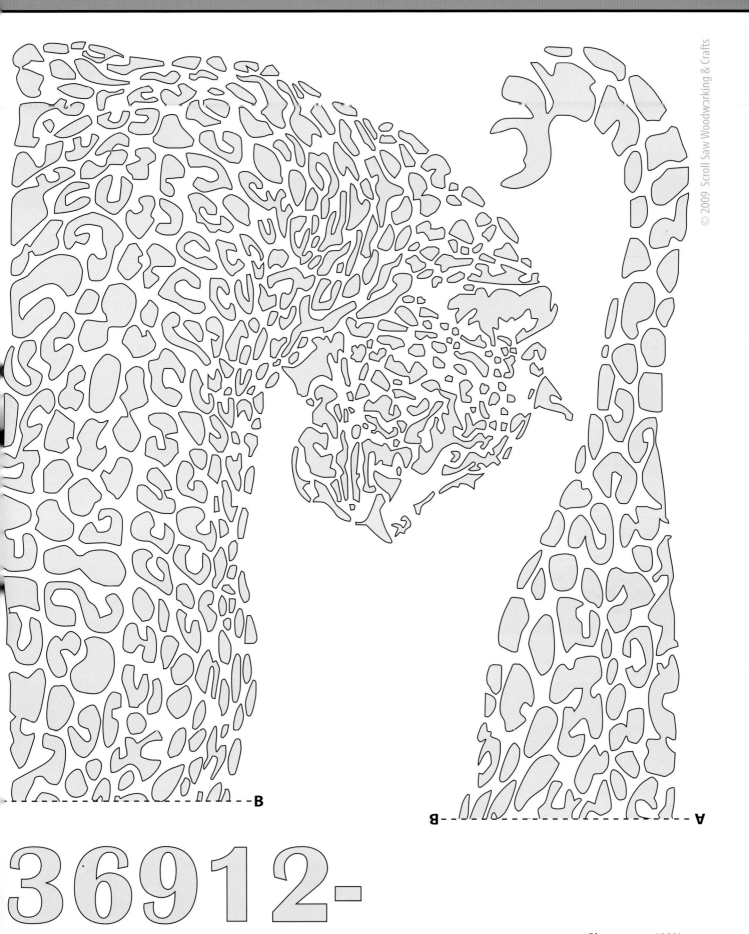

B

B

A

36912-

Photocopy at 100%

Romantic Stained-Glass Clock

Stack cut fretwork and segmentation sections for an elegant gift

By Kathy Wise

This graceful design looks complex, but simple stack-cutting techniques drastically reduce the production time. Both the fretwork and the segmentation portions are stack cut, providing a beautifully symmetrical project with a minimal amount of cutting.

Experiment with different colors of woods for a variety of distinctive looks. The pattern is identical for all four corners or panels of the project. For the sections with the white roses and dark background, use the bottom of the stock, or the opposite side that the pattern is on.

Cutting the fretwork

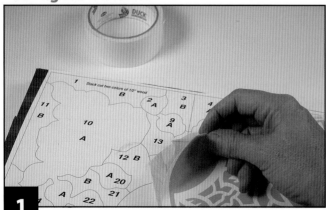

1 **Prepare the blanks for stack cutting.** Choose ½"-thick contrasting woods, and create two separate stacks using double-sided carpet tape. Attach the segmentation pattern to each stack. Stack four ¼"-thick pieces of plywood together, wrap masking tape around the edges, and attach the fretwork pattern.

2 **Cut the fretwork.** Drill blade entry holes for the frets with a ⅛"-diameter drill bit. For best results, use a drill press. Cut the frets with a #2 or #3 reverse-tooth blade. Separate the stack, remove the pattern, and sand both sides of each panel with 220-grit sandpaper.

Cutting the segmentation

3   **Cut the segmentation pieces.** Use a #2 or #3 reverse-tooth blade. Cut both stacks to produce four panels of segmentation work. Interchange the A and B sections and arrange the panels alternating dark and light roses. Two of the sections are mirror images of the pattern, so flip the pieces as needed.

4   **Glue the segmentation sections together.** Use cyanoacrylate (CA) glue to assemble each of the individual quarters. Do not glue the quarters together yet. Sand the top and bottom flat. Don't worry if the pieces don't fit exactly; the fretwork top layer will hide many of the flaws.

Staining and painting

5   **Prevent the white wood from yellowing.** Apply white gel stain to the white sections and immediately wipe it off. Do not get the stain on the darker wood. Carefully apply the gel near the edges; then wipe the stain towards the center of the white wood (away from the dark wood) with a clean cotton swab.

6   **Paint the fretwork black.** Apply a matte black spray paint on all four sides of the Baltic birch plywood. Instead of painted plywood, you could use a dark wood such as walnut or ebony. The dark fretwork mimics the lead beads in a stained-glass window. Make sure the inside of the cuts are painted as well.

Glue-up

7   **Glue the fretwork to the segmentation.** Apply several dots of CA glue along the perimeter and interior of the bottom of the fretwork. Carefully position the fretwork over the segmentation, and press it into place. Paint the outside edges of the segmentation matte black. Repeat for each panel.

8   **Prepare the backer board.** Trace around the assembled sections on ¼"-thick plywood. Cut ¼" inside the line. Center and cut the clock insert circle from the backer board. Paint the back of the board and approximately ½" around the front of the cut out circle with matte black spray paint.

Assembly and finish

9 **Assemble the project.** Apply wood glue to the front of the backing board. Add a few drops of CA glue to hold the pieces in place. Position the segmentation panels on the backing board, and press them in place. Align the sections as tightly as possible to eliminate any gaps. Let the glue dry overnight.

10 **Apply a finish to the clock.** Test the fit of the clock insert, and sand the center hole until the insert fits securely. Sand the outside edges flat if needed. Touch up any bare areas with black paint. Spray the finished clock with a clear satin varnish, and let it dry overnight. Add a hanger to the back and insert the clock.

© 2009 Scroll Saw Woodworking & Crafts

Fretwork Overlay
Stack 4 pieces

Photocopy at 100%

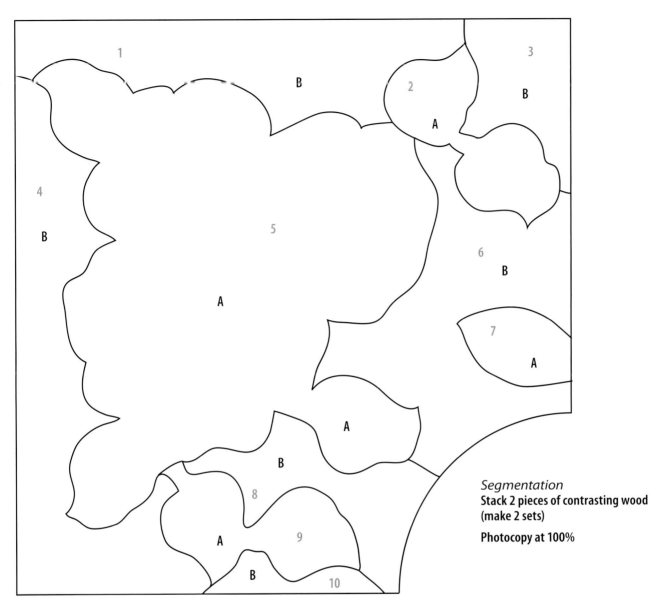

1

3

B

2

A

B

4

B

5

6

B

A

7

A

A

B

8

A

9

B

10

Segmentation

Stack 2 pieces of contrasting wood (make 2 sets)

Photocopy at 100%

Materials & Tools

Materials:

- 2 pieces ½" x 7" x 7" poplar or white wood of choice (white segmentation)
- 2 pieces ½" x 7" x 7" bloodwood or red wood of choice (red segmentation)
- 4 pieces ¼" x 7" x 7" Baltic birch plywood or dark wood of choice (fretwork)
- ¼" x 14" x 14" Baltic birch plywood (backing board)
- 4" (100mm)-diameter clock insert
- Spray adhesive
- Wood glue
- Clear satin spray varnish

- White-base gel varnish
- Wiping rags
- Mirror-type hanger
- Cyanoacrylate (CA) glue
- Matte black spray paint
- Double-sided carpet tape
- Cotton swabs
- Assorted grits of sandpaper up to 220-grit

Tools:

- #2 or #3 reverse-tooth blades or blades of choice
- Drill with ⅛"-diameter drill bit
- Paintbrush (to apply gel varnish)

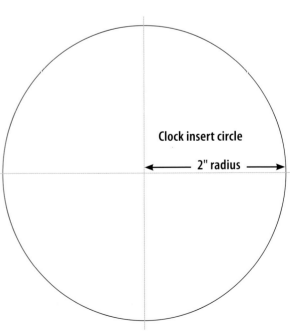

Clock insert circle

2" radius

Fretwork Shelf Clock

A vintage 1895 pattern

By John A. Nelson

This pattern is from an old Bowman and Russell catalog dated 1895. The Bowman and Russell Company sold scroll saw patterns and miscellaneous inside pieces such as clock movements. I liked the clock very much, so I made it into a scroll saw project for all of us to enjoy today. It has been modified slightly to fit a modern quartz insert. In the original clock, a small brass spring movement provided the power.

Modified from a pattern of a clock found in a Bowman and Russell catalog, the design was cut by Joe Diveley.

Step 1: Make copies of the patterns for the clock. Cut them apart and arrange the patterns on the wood in such a way that shows off the grain best, especially on the facing pieces, Parts 4, 5, 6, and 7. Cut all pieces to size per the parts list. Using fine sandpaper, lightly sand the top and bottom surfaces.

Step 2: Adhere the patterns. Spray the patterns with temporary bond adhesive and attach them to the wood.

Step 3: Cut the front and back. The front and back (Part 6) are nearly identical. The back has a round opening, and the front, a scalloped square opening at the center. Cut them out individually, or to save time, stack cut the front and back pieces. To prepare the stack, use three small brads to temporarily nail the back and front pieces together. Put the nails in the rounded, cutout area of the back and later, when you cut out the round hole in the back, the nail holes will be eliminated. You might want to tape the outer edges also, so no movement whatsoever is possible between the pieces.

CHOOSING WOODS   TIP

The really fun part about making any project is looking for ways to let your personality show through. I purposely did not specify wood choices for this clock. My suggestion is to use the woods that are locally available. They tend to be less expensive than special orders from another part of the country. A simple guideline to follow is to choose woods that have interesting, attractive grain patterns. For this particular clock, I like to use dark wood for the majority of its construction, with light wood used as accents in Parts 7 and 8, as well as Part 5. If you can't find contrasting wood, you can stain the pieces you'd like to use as accents.

Step 4: Drill blade entry holes. They should be ¹⁄₃₂" to ¹⁄₁₆" in diameter in all interior areas. Make all interior cuts with a #2 blade. Cut out the exterior last, again using the #2. (Always make interior cuts first as doing so gives you material to hang on to, thus more control.) Take the two pieces apart and cut out the scalloped square area in the front, then cut out the round hole in the back piece. Carefully sand all over to remove burrs.

Step 5: Glue Parts 1, 2, and 3. Make up the box assembly as shown, using Parts 1, 2 and 3. I like to use CA glue because it dries in 30 seconds, making clamps unnecessary. Be sure to keep the bottom section at exactly 90 degrees.

Step 6: Fit Part 4 (Face) to the box assembly. Using the CA glue, attach it in place ¼" in from the front surface (see drawing). This placement is important because it creates extra depth.

Step 7: Attach Part 5 (Trim) to Part 4 (Face).

Step 8: Attach the front and back pieces. Affix Part 6 to the box assembly.

Step 9: Attach Part 7 (Trim) to the box assembly. Use small brass brads. You also can glue it in place with the Super "T." The original would have been nailed together.

Step 10: Glue Part 8 (Roof Trim) to the box assembly. Note that it butts up against Part 7 (Trim) so glue it to Part 7 also.

Step 11: Finish using your favorite finish. I like a simple clear tung oil finish—no stain—and a satin finish. If you used a nice hardwood that has an attractive grain pattern, tung oil will make a nice finish. To complete the project, apply four padded felt feet on the bottom.

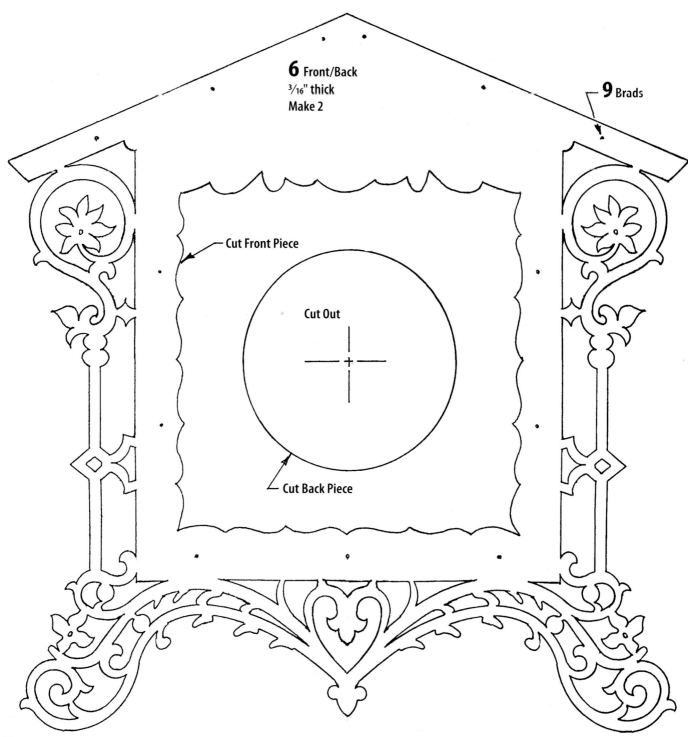

6 Front/Back
3/16" thick
Make 2

9 Brads

Cut Front Piece

Cut Out

Cut Back Piece

Photocopy at 125%

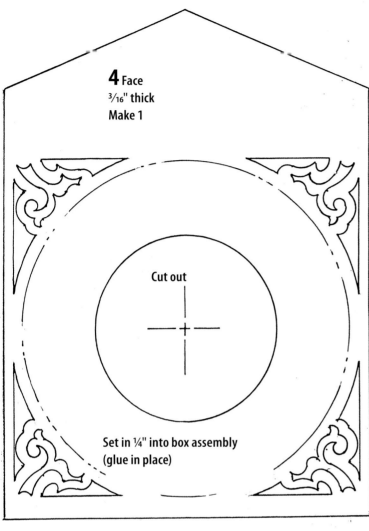

4 Face
³⁄₁₆" thick
Make 1

Cut out

Set in ¼" into box assembly
(glue in place)

Photocopy at 125%

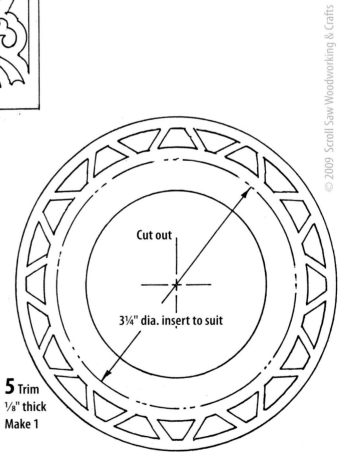

Cut out

3¼" dia. insert to suit

5 Trim
¹⁄₈" thick
Make 1

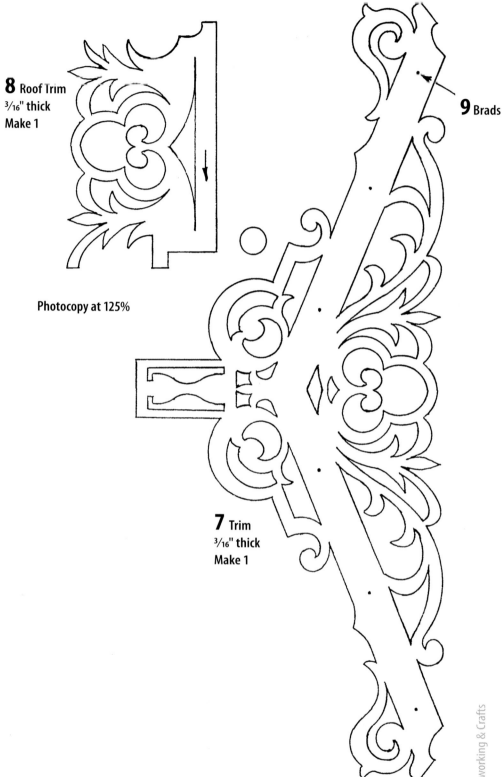

8 Roof Trim
³/₁₆" thick
Make 1

9 Brads

Photocopy at 125%

7 Trim
³/₁₆" thick
Make 1

23°

Material: ³⁄₁₆" thick
3" wide

5⁹⁄₁₆"

①

②

Box Assembly

③

¼"

①

④

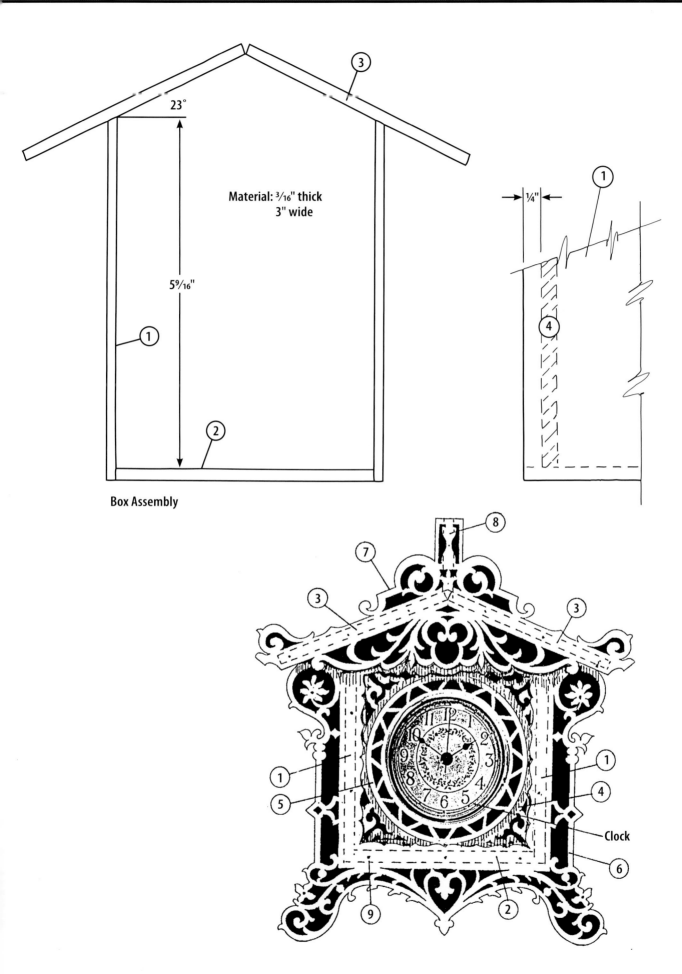

Clock

Gingerbread Wall Clock

Delicate fretwork designs highlight this functional project

By John A. Nelson
Cut by Ben Fink

Handcrafted items make popular gifts. Stack cut the individual parts of this elegant clock to cut several projects at once.

Different wood can really alter the appearance of the project. This clock was made with red oak, but feel free to choose stock to complement your décor.

Take caution to orient the long narrow sections, such as the top and pendulum backer, with the grain of the wood. After cutting your materials to the rough dimensions listed in the materials list, attach the patterns to the blanks, drill blade entry holes and the ⅜"-diameter hole for the clock movement. Cut out the fretwork and use sandpaper to remove any rough edges.

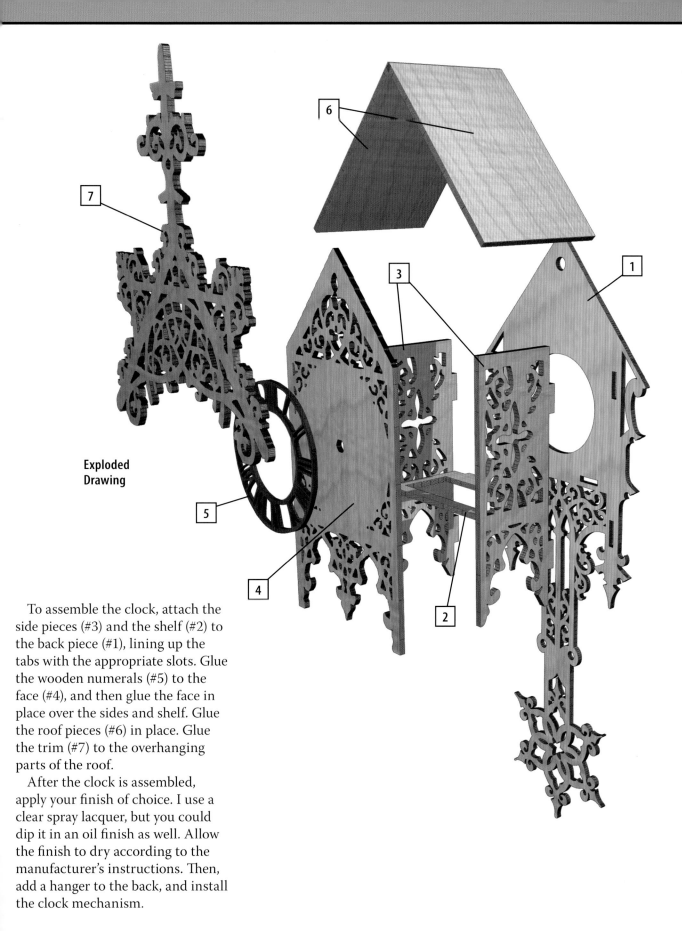

Exploded Drawing

To assemble the clock, attach the side pieces (#3) and the shelf (#2) to the back piece (#1), lining up the tabs with the appropriate slots. Glue the wooden numerals (#5) to the face (#4), and then glue the face in place over the sides and shelf. Glue the roof pieces (#6) in place. Glue the trim (#7) to the overhanging parts of the roof.

After the clock is assembled, apply your finish of choice. I use a clear spray lacquer, but you could dip it in an oil finish as well. Allow the finish to dry according to the manufacturer's instructions. Then, add a hanger to the back, and install the clock mechanism.

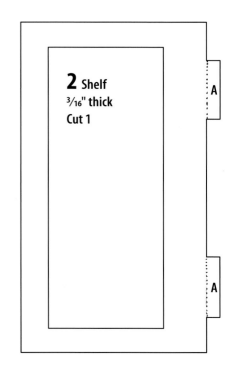

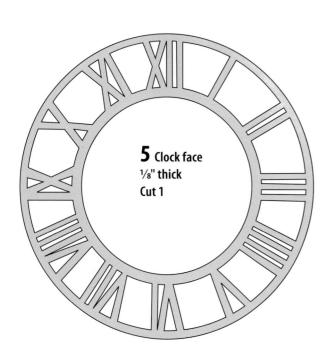

5 Clock face
⅛" thick
Cut 1

2 Shelf
³⁄₁₆" thick
Cut 1

A

A

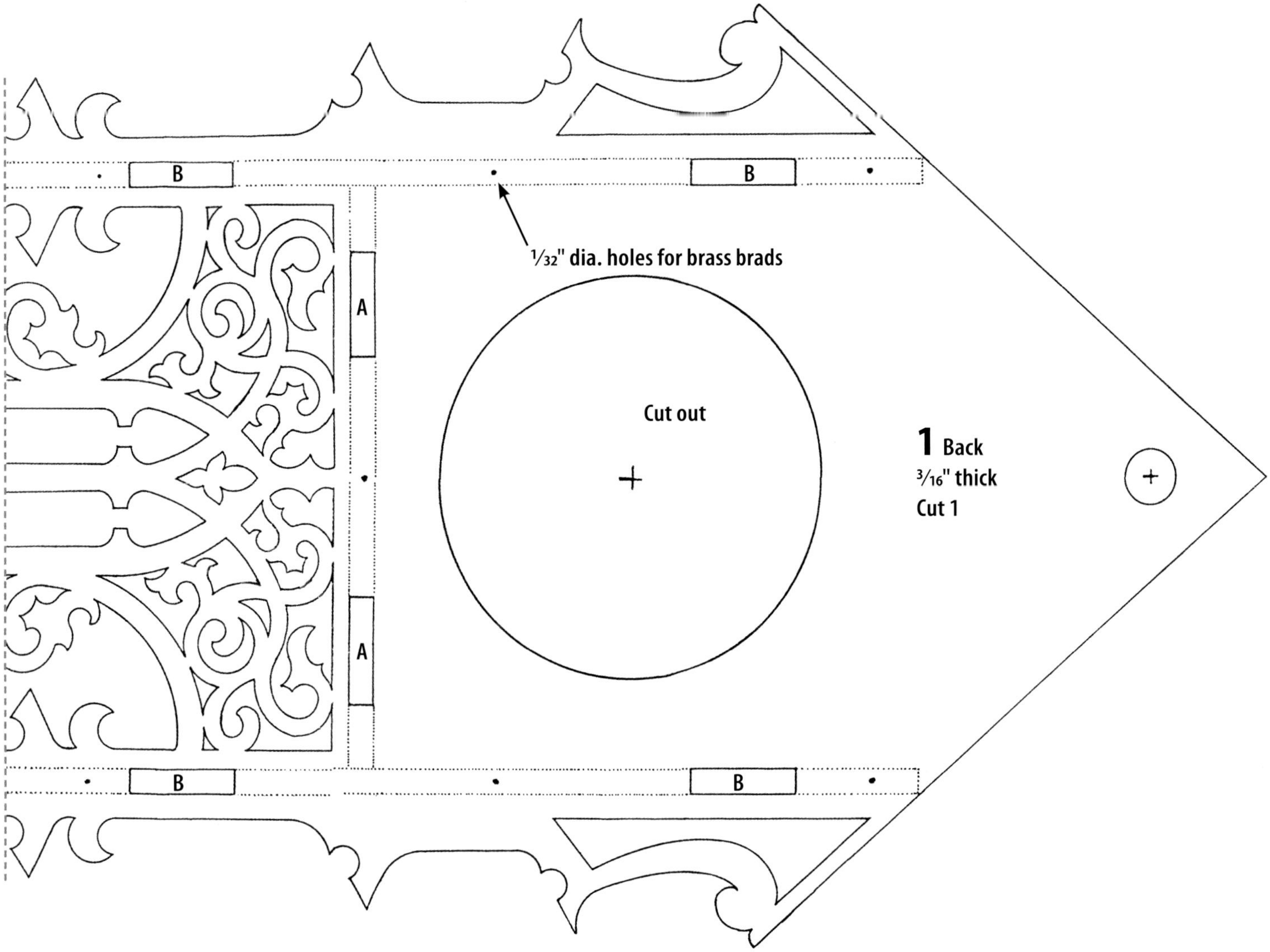

¹/₃₂" dia. holes for brass brads

B

B

A

A

Cut out

+

1 Back
³/₁₆" thick
Cut 1

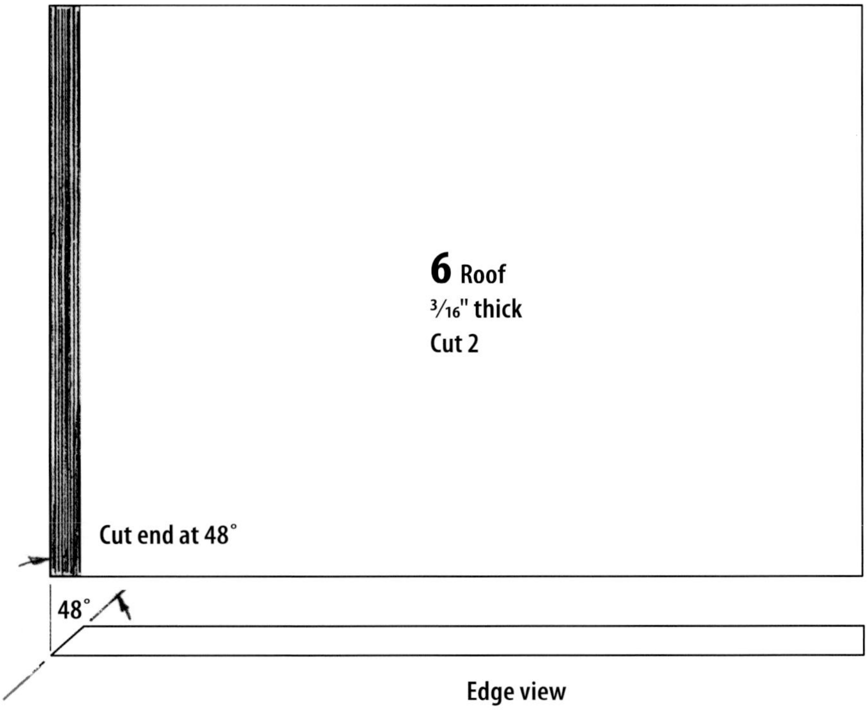

+

B

B

6 Roof
³/₁₆" thick
Cut 2

Cut end at 48°

48°

Edge view

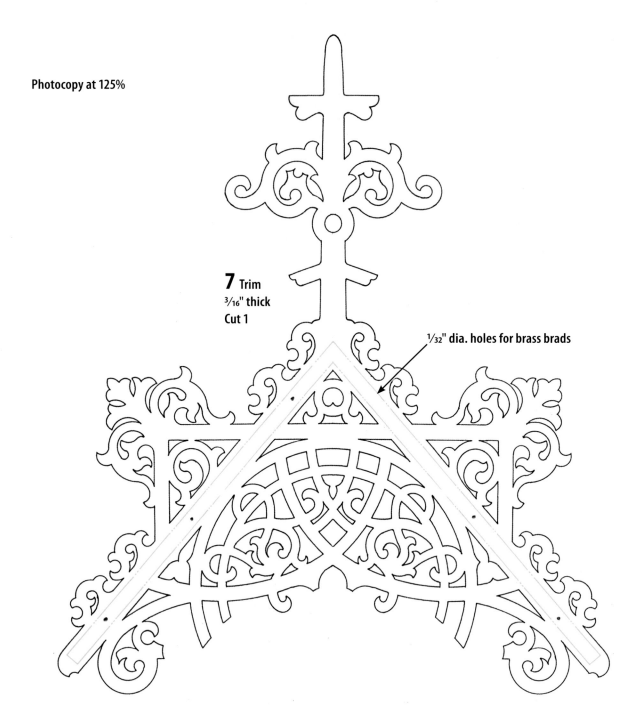

7 Trim
³⁄₁₆" thick
Cut 1

¹⁄₃₂" dia. holes for brass brads

Photocopy at 125%

4 Face
³/₁₆" thick
Cut 1

⁵/₁₆" dia. hole

B

B

3 Side
³/₁₆" thick
Cut 2

¹/₃₂" dia. holes for brass brads

Japanese Mantel Clock

Stylized herons adorn this original antique timepiece

By John A. Nelson

Scrollers looking for their next challenge often turn to complicated fretwork clocks. The tight turns and sharp corners require superior cutting technique and will set your work apart from other scrollers'. And the payoff is tremendous. The compliments one receives for a nicely done fretwork clock are absolutely priceless.

If you're looking for a pattern to put you through your paces, try your hand at making this mantel clock. It's based on a Russell catalog pattern, which back in 1895 cost a whopping 15 cents. I tried to stay true to the original pattern, but I did modify it slightly to accommodate a modern quartz movement with a pendulum. As with any delicate fretwork, straight-grained hardwoods such as mahogany, cherry, and maple are excellent choices. These woods are both beautiful and strong. These traits are especially important if you're going to give the clock as a gift or sell it at a craft show.

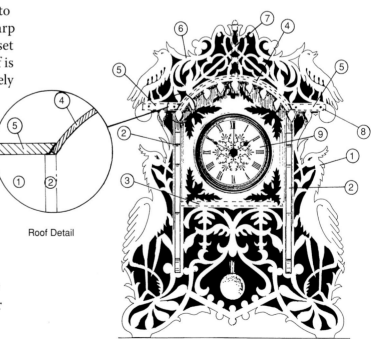

Roof Detail

Assembly View

With any type of project requiring assembly, it's important to fit each piece to its mating part as you go. Be sure to make all notches just a little wider than the thickness of the wood. You want a snug fit but not too tight of a fit.

Step 1: Understand the plans. Before starting, be sure you completely understand how the clock goes together. Make any adjustments to the pattern prior to making copies. These adjustments may be due to using ¼"-thick wood instead of the ³⁄₁₆" called for or using clock parts slightly different from the ones I used.

Step 2: Cut all pieces of wood to overall size. Try to make sure all corners are 90°. Sand the top and bottom surfaces with fine sandpaper.

Step 3: Make copies of all patterns. Cut out the individual pattern parts, allowing about a ¾" margin around each pattern's outside lines.

Step 4: Attach the patterns to the wood using spray adhesive. Take care to put the adhesive spray on the pattern and not the wood so the glue doesn't get into the grain.

Stack cut the front and back pieces to save time. You can also stack cut the two sides. To make the stack, simply line up the wood and tape the pieces together using masking tape around the outside edges of the wood. Attach the patterns to the top of the stack. The front and back pieces are not exactly the same, so glue the front pattern to the stack, and make all the cuts that are in the back piece, except the notch and the large hole. Separate the pieces and continue cutting the front piece. On the back piece cut out the notch and large hole.

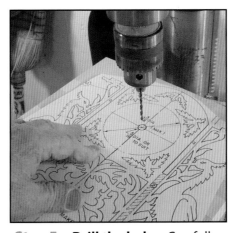

Step 5: Drill the holes. Carefully drill all blade entry holes with the ⅛"-diameter drill bit. Use the ¹⁄₁₆"-diameter bit in small areas.

Step 6: Remove burrs. Sand the back with medium-grit sandpaper to remove all the burrs from drilling, so the wood won't get hung up on the saw table as you make turns and cuts.

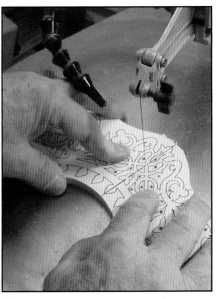

Step 7: Cut the parts. When I design my projects, I draw the patterns and number them to represent the best order for assembly. I encourage you to cut the parts in numerical sequence so adjustments can be made to parts that connect to each other. Make all interior cuts with a #2 blade. Cut the slots with a #9 blade. Finish up by cutting the exterior cuts with the #2 blade.

Step 8: Make the center roof arc. The best method is to shape a piece of wood by clamping it in a wood block. To use this method, get some scrap wood and glue it up to make a block approximately 3" x 4" x 6". Cut the block into two pieces with an arc equal to the one shown on the roof center pattern. Soak a piece of wood ⅛" thick x 3" x about 6" long overnight, and put it in between the block pieces. Clamp for 12 hours.

The second option is to cut four arcs out of ¾"-thick wood and glue them together, using the pattern provided. Sand the pieces. The third method is to make these from 1⁄16"-thick plywood. Bend to the shape at assembly.

Step 9: Cut the roof sidepieces. Saw the roof sidepieces and the two notches. Check the fit with front and back pieces.

Step 10: Complete all pieces. Finish all pieces and sand with fine-grit sandpaper. Wipe all pieces to remove all dust. Add stain and finish.

Step 11: Dry-fit all pieces. Trim to fit if necessary.

Step 12: Assemble the case. Glue the case together, taking care to keep everything square. If using CA glue, make sure you use it in a well-ventilated room.

Step 13: Apply the finish. Carefully add a coat of paste wax for a satin smooth finish.

Step 14: Check out the clock instructions. Completely check all clock components. Read the instructions that come with the clock dial face and movement, and assemble per the directions.

Step 15: Put it all together. Attach the clock dial face and movement to the case using a center shaft nut and washer. Add batteries and you're done. Enjoy.

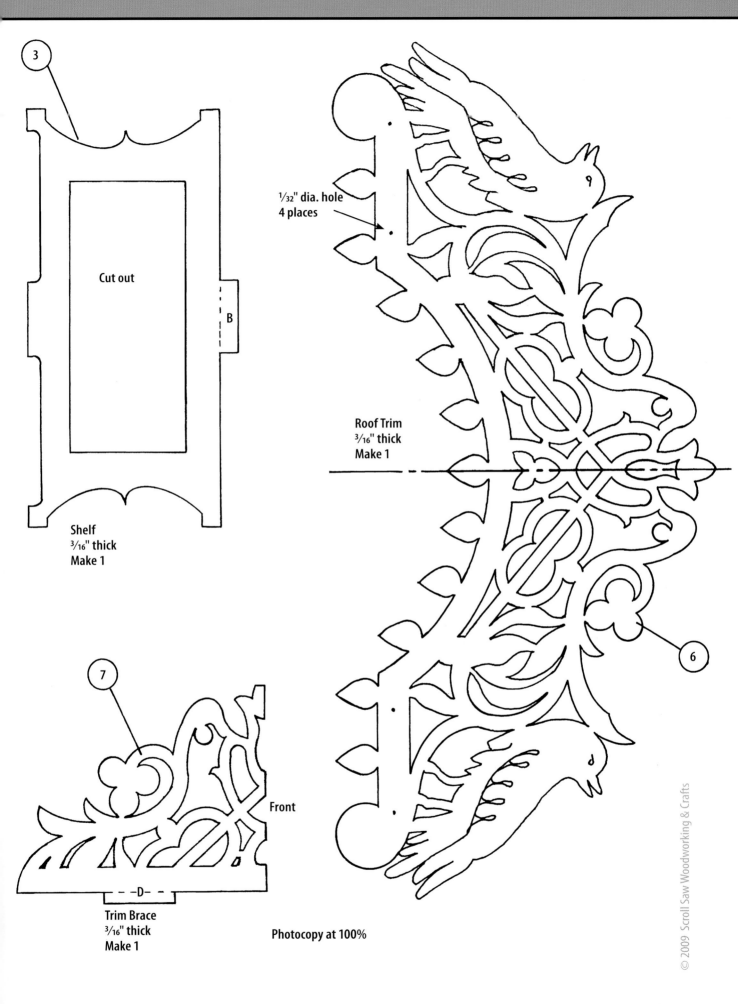

3

Cut out

B

Shelf
³⁄₁₆" thick
Make 1

¹⁄₃₂" dia. hole
4 places

Roof Trim
³⁄₁₆" thick
Make 1

6

7

Front

−D−

Trim Brace
³⁄₁₆" thick
Make 1

Photocopy at 100%

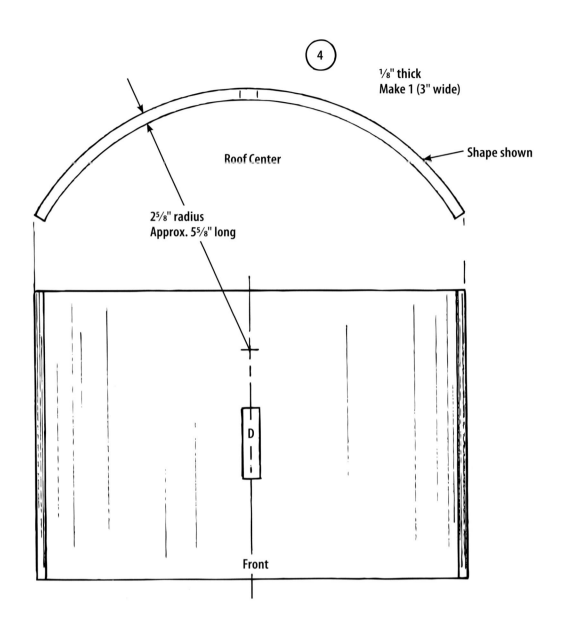

(4)

⅛" thick
Make 1 (3" wide)

Shape shown

Roof Center

2⅝" radius
Approx. 5⅝" long

D

Front

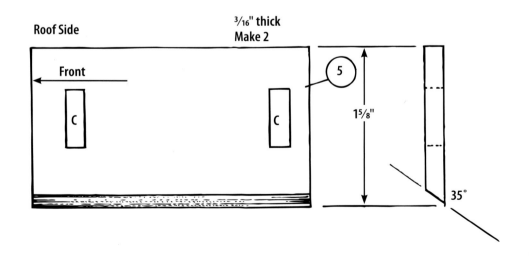

Roof Side

³⁄₁₆" thick
Make 2

Front

C

C

(5)

1⅝"

35°

Materials & Tools

Materials:
- ³⁄₁₆" x 9¼" x 10⅝" straight-grained hardwood of choice (Part 1-Front)
- ³⁄₁₆" x 9¼" x 10⅝" (Part 1a-Back)
- 2 pieces, ³⁄₁₆" x 3¼" x 6½" (Part 2-Side)
- ³⁄₁₆" x 2¼" x 4⅜" (Part 3-Shelf)
- ⅛" x 3" x 5⅝" (Part 4-Roof Arc)
- 2 pieces, ³⁄₁₆" x 1⅝" x 3" (Part 5-Roof Sides)
- ³⁄₁₆" x 4¼" x 9" (Part 6-Roof Trim)
- ³⁄₁₆" x 2⅛" x 2¾" (Part 7-Roof Brace)
- 4 each, ⅝" long brads (Part 8, optional)
- Dial, 3⅜" (Part 9)
- Hands (Part 10)
- Movement (Part 11)
- 5½"-long Pendulum (Part 12)
- 2"-diameter Brass Bob (Part 13)
- Temporary bond spray adhesive
- Masking tape
- Sandpaper, medium and fine grits
- Cyanoacrylate (CA) glue

Tools:
- #2 and #9 skip-tooth blades
- Drill with ¹⁄₁₆"-, ⅛"-, and ⁵⁄₁₆"-diameter bits

Photocopy at 100%

Side
³⁄₁₆" thick
Make 2

Slot

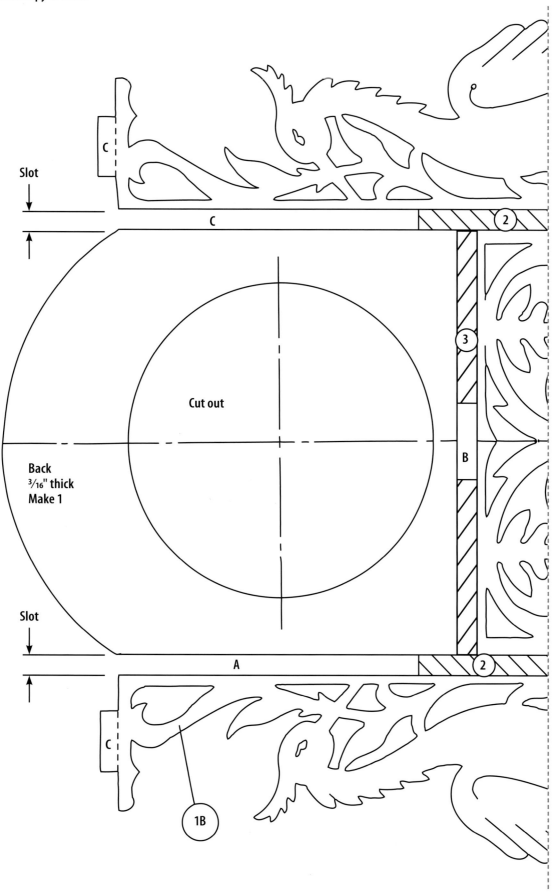

Slot

C

Cut out

Back
³/₁₆" thick
Make 1

Slot

C

A

B

3

2

2

1B

Back

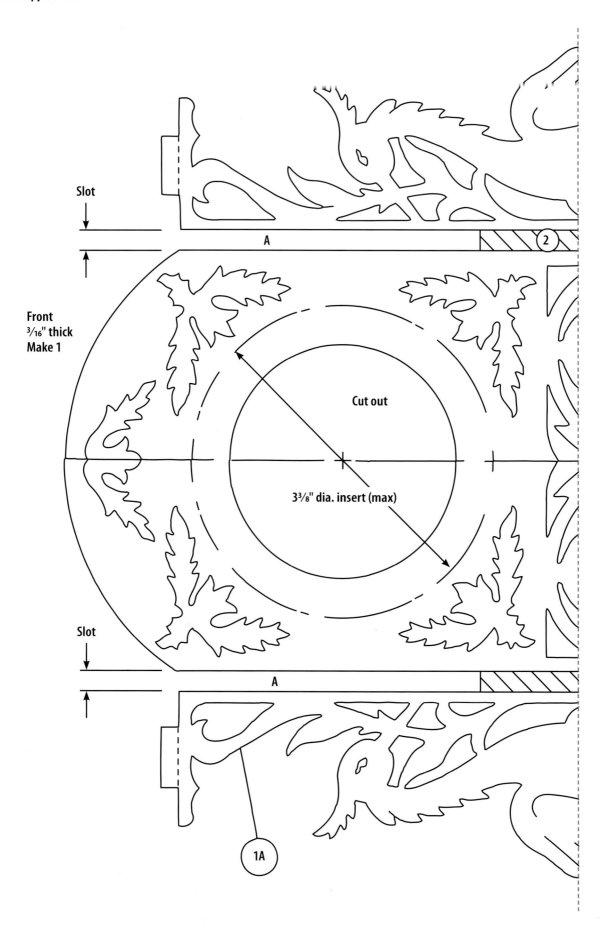

Slot

Front
3/16" thick
Make 1

Slot

A

A

2

Cut out

3³⁄₈" dia. insert (max)

1A

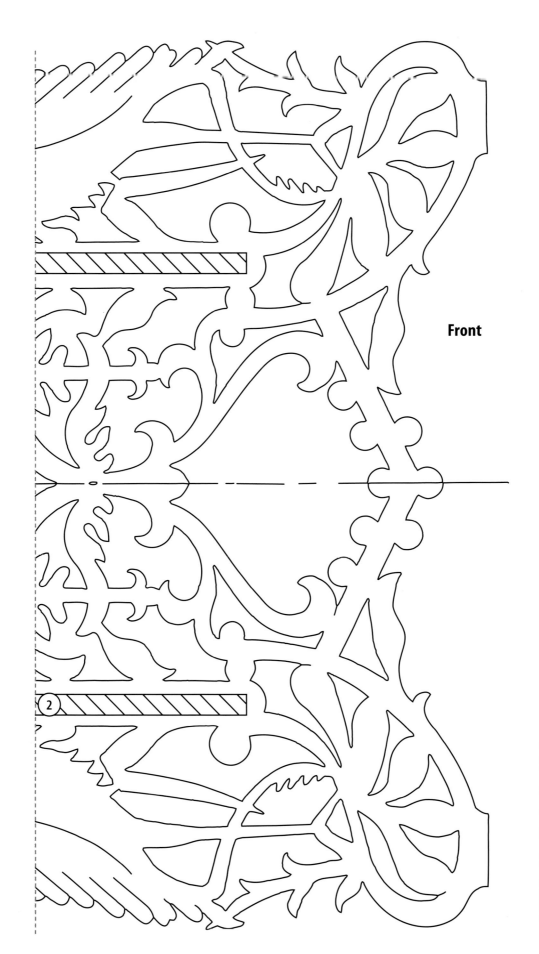

Front

②

Windmill
Clock

Detailed fretwork highlights this impressive clock
By Pedro Lopez
Cut by Ben Fink

This project was inspired by a photo I found printed in an English magazine from 1915. I get a lot of enjoyment from bringing historic patterns back to life and combining my hobbies of scrolling and working on the computer.

I did make some slight alterations to the windmill clock, such as adding a fifth blade. I hope that today's scrollers enjoy crafting my version of this historic project.

Step 1: Prepare the wood. This project is designed for ⅛"-thick wood. Be sure to match the slot thickness to the wood you are using. Several of the pieces can be stack cut, which gives you better control when cutting the thin wood and produces perfectly identical pieces. Start by cutting the pieces to size and attaching the parts to be stack cut.

Step 2: Drill the blade entry holes. Use a ⅟₁₆"-diameter drill bit. It is best to drill the holes with a drill press to ensure they are perpendicular to your stock.

Step 3: Cut the parts. Use a #1 reverse-tooth blade when cutting single pieces, and a #3 or #5 reverse-tooth blade when stack cutting, depending on the stack thickness. Slow down your saw speed for maximum accuracy. Cut the interior frets of each piece before the perimeter. I cut the ¾"-thick rotation spacer with a #3 blade.

Step 4: Prepare for assembly. Sand the pieces with 220-grit sandpaper. Dry fit the pieces together to make sure they fit properly. Make adjustments as needed. Use the exploded drawing as a guide.

Step 5: Assemble the main body. Because it dries quickly, I use cyanoacrylate (CA) glue. Start with the base (parts C and D) and work your way toward the top. Note that part E forms the outside ribs that

match part I, resulting in five ribs along the front and back of the clock. Part I is also slotted into part E on each side.

▲ **Step 6: Assemble the blade hub.** Glue part S to the front of part R and then glue this assembly to the front of part J. The windmill blade assembly will rotate on part S.

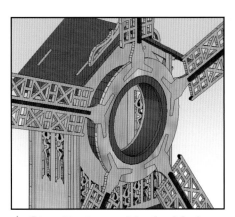

▲ **Step 7: Assemble the blades.** Assemble the individual blades (part U and part T), then glue the blades onto part PA. Fit this blade assembly onto part S. Do not glue the assembly in place. Make sure part PA rotates easily on part S.

▲ **Step 8: Lock the blade assembly in place.** Glue part Q to the rim of part S. Be careful not to allow the glue to squeeze out onto the blade assembly.

Step 9: Finish the clock. I use a spray lacquer to finish the project after assembly. Apply your finish of choice according to the manufacturer's directions. When dry, add the clock insert to complete the project.

SIZING THE SLOTS | TIP

Use a scrap of wood the same thickness as your stock to mark the slots. This will compensate if your wood thickness happens to differ from the slots drawn on the pattern.

Exploded Drawing

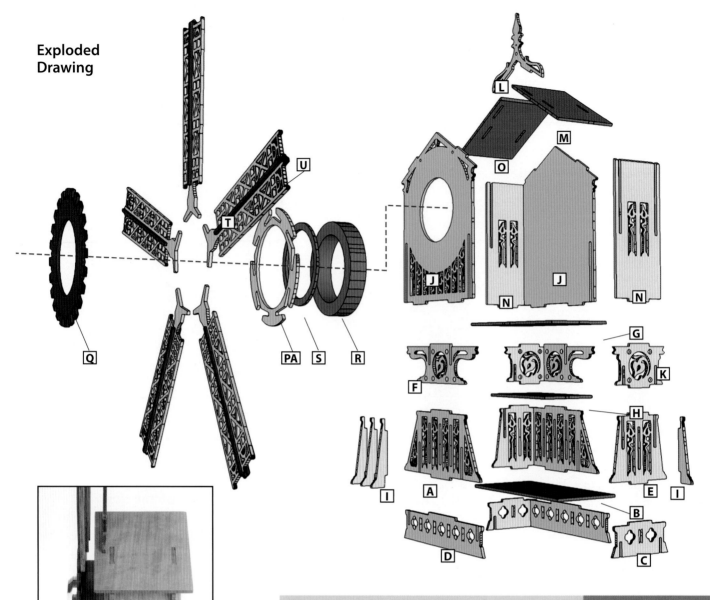

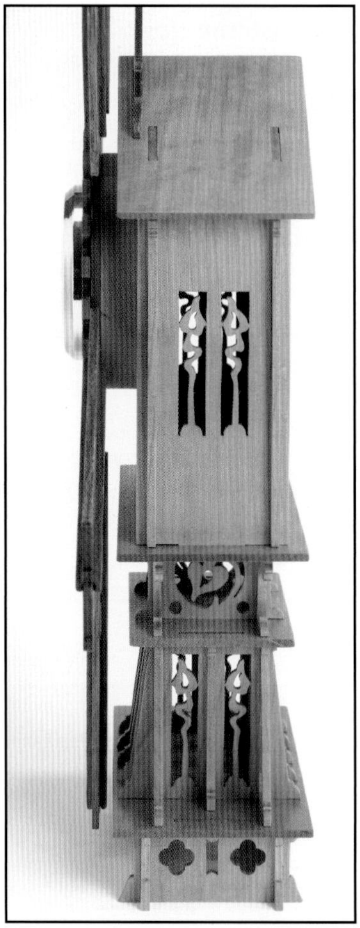

Materials:

Wood of choice: (Test cutter Ben Fink used cherry and walnut)

- 2 pieces ⅛" x 3" x 6½" (A)
- ⅛" x 3½" x 6¾" (B)
- 2 pieces ⅛" x 1½" x 3¼" (C)
- 2 pieces ⅛" x 1½" x 6¾" (D)
- 2 pieces ⅛" x 3" x 3¼" (E)
- 2 pieces ⅛" x 1¾" x 6" (F)
- ⅛" x 3¼" x 6¾" (G)
- ⅛" x 3" x 4½" (H)
- 2 pieces ⅛" x 2¾" x 3¼" (I)
- 2 pieces ⅛" x 6½" x 7¾" (J)
- 2 pieces ⅛" x 2" x 3" (K)
- ⅛" x 3½" x 4¼" (L)

- 2 pieces ⅛" x 3¼" x 4¼" (M, O)
- 2 pieces ⅛" x 3½" x 6" (N)
- ⅛" x 5" x 5" (P or PA)
- ⅛" x 5¼" x 5¼" (Q)
- ⅛" x 3½" x 3½" (S)
- 4 or 5 pieces ⅛" x 2¼" x 8" (T)
- 4 or 5 pieces ⅛" x ½" x 6¾" (U)
- ¾" x 4" x 4" pine or wood of choice (R)
- Assorted grits of sandpaper
- Cyanoacrylate (CA) glue

Materials & Tools

- Finish of choice (I use spray lacquer)
- 3⁵⁄₁₆" (83mm)-diameter clock insert

Tools:

- #1, #3 & #5 reverse-tooth blades or blades of choice
- Sanding sticks or needle files

Photocopy at 125%

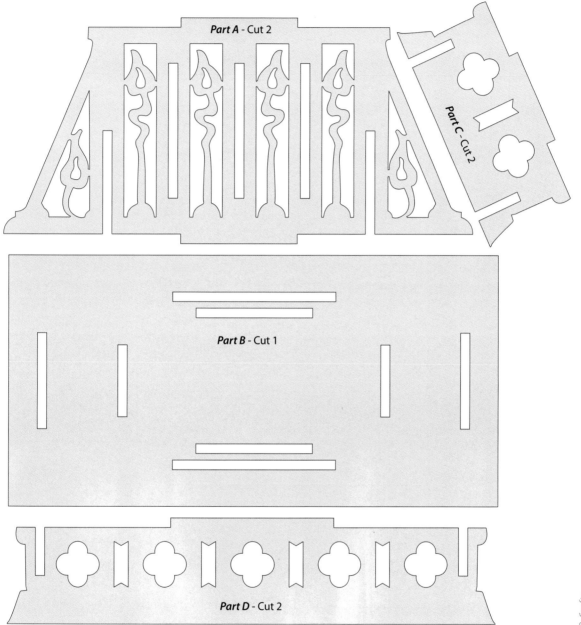

Part A - Cut 2

Part C - Cut 2

Part B - Cut 1

Part D - Cut 2

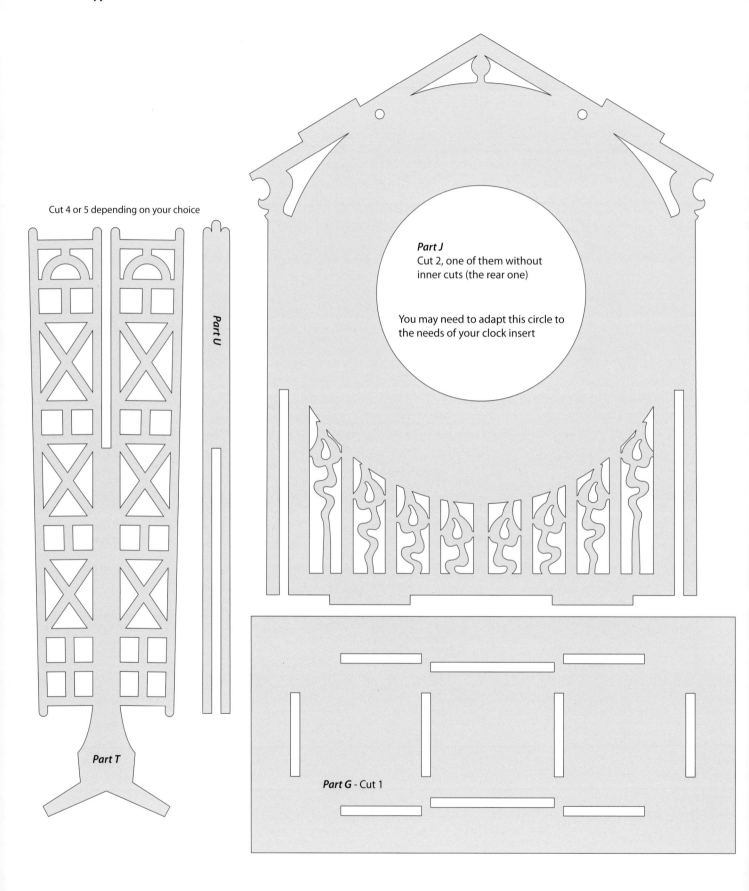

Cut 4 or 5 depending on your choice

Part U

Part J
Cut 2, one of them without inner cuts (the rear one)

You may need to adapt this circle to the needs of your clock insert

Part T

Part G - Cut 1

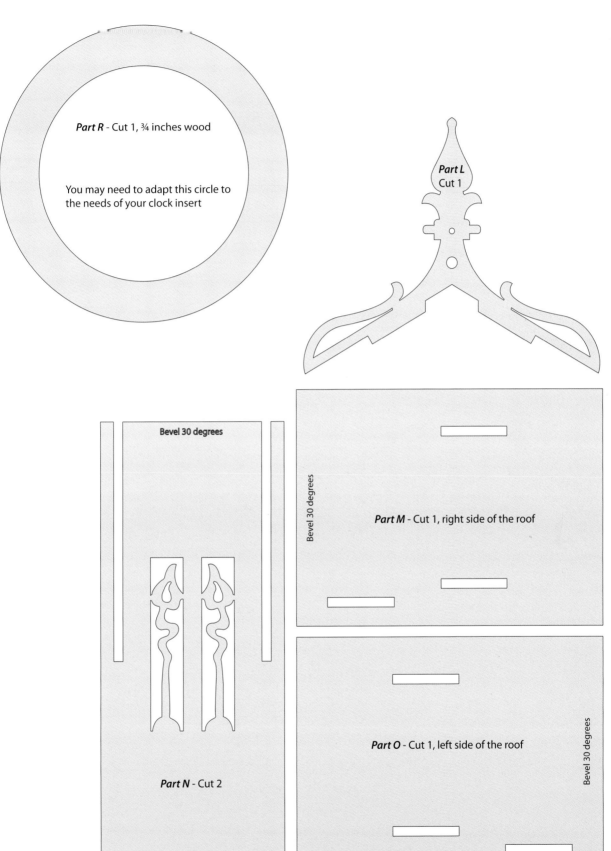

Part R - Cut 1, ¾ inches wood

You may need to adapt this circle to the needs of your clock insert

Part L
Cut 1

Bevel 30 degrees

Bevel 30 degrees

Part M - Cut 1, right side of the roof

Bevel 30 degrees

Part O - Cut 1, left side of the roof

Part N - Cut 2

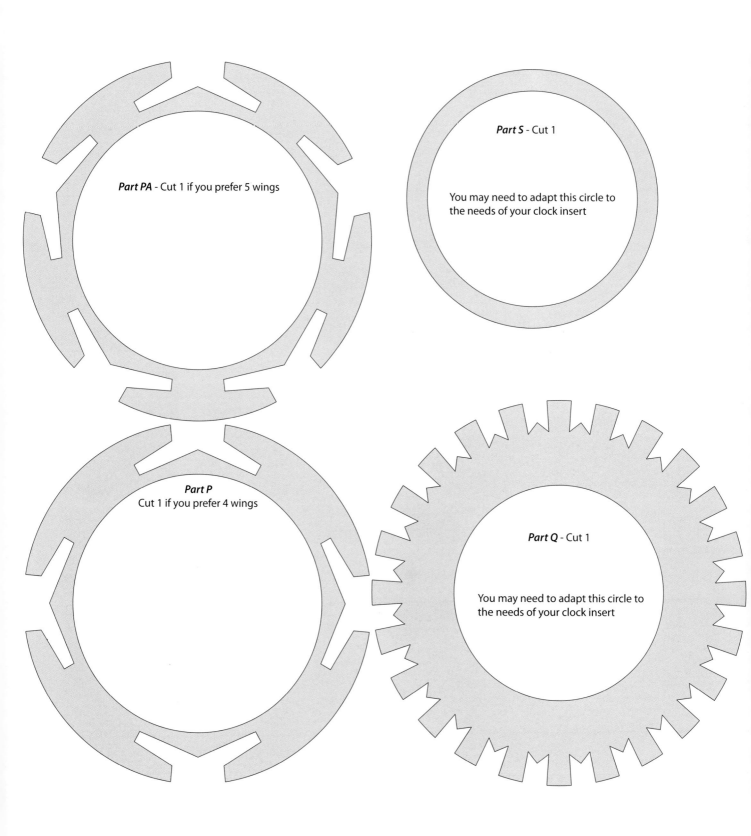

Part PA - Cut 1 if you prefer 5 wings

Part S - Cut 1

You may need to adapt this circle to the needs of your clock insert

Part P
Cut 1 if you prefer 4 wings

Part Q - Cut 1

You may need to adapt this circle to the needs of your clock insert

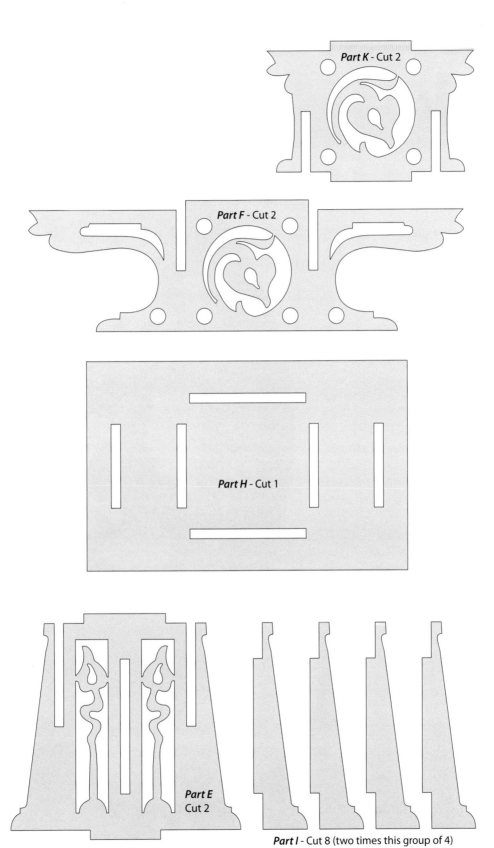

Part K - Cut 2

Part F - Cut 2

Part H - Cut 1

Part E
Cut 2

Part I - Cut 8 (two times this group of 4)

Wooden Gear Clock

Scroll a fully functional, 30-hour timepiece

By Marc Tovar

Once assembled, this wooden gear clock is an impressive work of art. When visitors discover that it runs without the aid of a battery and that you crafted it yourself, they will be truly amazed.

If you can bring yourself to part with it, the MLT-13 clock makes a wonderful gift for the individual who already owns just about everything. Don't be surprised if the completed timepiece initiates a few custom commissions!

When cutting out the parts for the MLT-13, it is very important that you make accurate cuts. This is especially true when you are cutting out the leaves of the pinions and the teeth of the wheels. If these are not cut accurately, the clock will not work. If you are not confident in your cutting ability, cut to the waste side of the lines and sand or file up to the lines.

Study the exploded drawing/assembly diagram and the patterns until you are familiar with them. The patterns will refer back to the exploded drawing for assembling the parts. All of the patterns are drafted with the pieces facing towards you. Material thicknesses are noted on the patterns. For a project this intricate that has so many delicate parts, use Baltic birch plywood for everything. The plywood will hold up much longer than hardwood teeth and leaves.

Prepare the Pieces

Step 1: Transfer the patterns to all of the blanks. Copy the pattern, apply spray adhesive to the back of the copies, and press them onto the wood. DO NOT use carbon or graphite paper. Accuracy is critically important.

Step 2: Drill the holes where indicated on the pattern. Use a brad-point drill bit. For the %4"-diameter holes, drill first with a ⅛"-diameter brad-point bit. Then, re-drill the hole with a %4"-diameter bit (brad-point bits are not sized at %4").

Step 3: Cut out all of the pieces. Sand the pieces lightly to remove any rough edges.

Step 4: Apply the finish. Mix aniline dyes with denatured alcohol according to the dye manufacturer's instructions. Dye the individual pieces following my example or choose your own colors. Apply several coats of shellac to all of the surfaces except on the teeth and leaves. Varnishes and shellacs create too much friction in the teeth and leaves, and your clock will have a difficult time running. You may want to wait to apply the shellac after individual pieces are glued together, but before assembly.

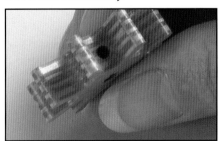

Assemble the Hands, Weights, and Axles

Step 5: Glue the collars onto the back of the hands. Then, drill a ⅛"-diameter hole between the hand and the collar into the axle hole for the set screw. At the same time, drill a ⅛"-diameter hole between two leaves on the edge of all of the pinions. This is for inserting a drop or two of shellac to bind the pinion to the axle.

Step 6: Make three leather plugs for the hands. I punch them out from a leather belt using a piece of ⁵⁄₃₂"-diameter tubing. They will be inserted in the holes drilled in step 5.

Step 7: Make the weight. Cut a 7"-long piece of 1½"-diameter thin-wall PVC pipe. Cut the wooden plugs for both ends, and sand them to fit tightly inside the pipe. Insert the bottom plug, and drill the holes for the ⅛"-diameter pins through the pipe into the plug. Drive the pins into place. Thread the ⅛"-diameter brass rod through the hole in the center of the bottom plug and fill the weight with #7½ lead shot. Put the top plug into place, with the brass rod threaded through the center hole, and drill the holes for the pins through the pipe into the plug. Then, drive the pins into place. Bend the ⅛"-diameter brass rod to shape.

Step 8: Make the counter weight. Drill two holes into the ⅜"-diameter dowel where indicated on the pattern. Then, taper the tip of the counterweight using a sander until it matches the pattern.

Step 9: Cut the pins, axles, and spacers to size. Use a hacksaw or a rotary power carver equipped with a carbide cutting disc. Remove any rough edges with a file and 400-grit wet/dry sandpaper. Use a small round file to remove any burrs from the inside of the spacer tubing. All the axles need to be burnished. To burnish the axles, mount them into a drill, and lightly sand them with 400-grit wet/dry sandpaper. Glue the sandpaper to two sticks and use these sticks to squeeze the axle as it turns. Continue sanding until the axle has a high gloss and no longer grips the sticks.

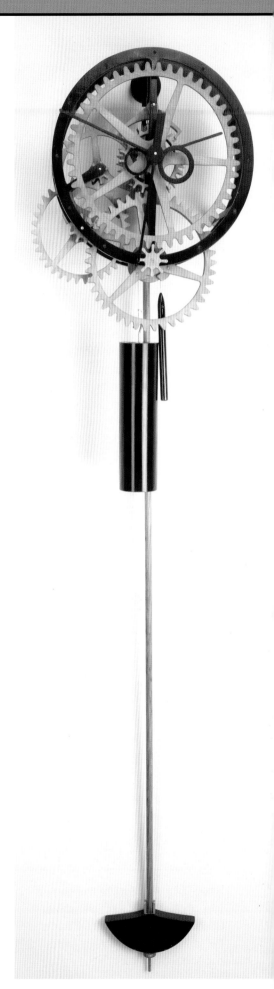

and the spacer between the CP and the EW. You must be able to insert the tube into the bore with hand pressure. It must be a snug fit. Glue the escape wheel pinion to the EW. The EW is mounted in the center of the clock. The CP is on the backside of F1. Insert the escape wheel arbor through the CP arbor, through the EW, the escape wheel pinion, EW spacer, and into the back frame. This will be a tight fit, and you may have to attach a hand drill to the tip of the arbor and screw it in through the EW.

Assemble the Clock

Step 10: Assemble the frame. F1, F2, and the ribs make up the frame. The ribs are marked with numbers that are the same as on the dial of a clock. Glue and clamp ribs 12, 4, and 8 onto the F1 and F2 frames. After they dry, glue the rest of the ribs into their respective spots. With a ⅛"-diameter bit, drill into the ends of the ribs, and dowel them to the frame. These dowels reinforce the strength of the frame. Drill small divets as hour markers where ribs do not join the two frames. Note: Rib 8 is attached to F2 only and does not require a dowel pin. Glue the wall anchor (WA) on the end of rib 12. Insert the ⅛"-diameter anchor pins into ribs 4 and 8.

Step 12: Add the clock hands and the hour wheel. The hour wheel has a ³⁄₁₆"-diameter brass tube as its axle. The hour hand is installed on this axle in front of the hour wheel. The hour wheel is installed in front of the frame and onto the CP tube. The minute hand is installed on the CP tube in front of the hour hand, and the second hand is installed on the EW axle. Be sure there is enough space between the hands to prevent them from touching each other. Lock the hands in place by screwing a ⅛"-diameter set screw through the holes between the hand and collar until the leather plug grips the axle.

Step 11: Assemble the canon pinion (CP) and escape wheel (EW) mechanism. The CP has a ⁵⁄₃₂"-diameter bore for the brass tube that acts as both the arbor

Step 13: Insert the clicker brass pins into the great wheel (GW). The pins will stick out the back of the GW. The clickers (C) are mounted onto these pins. The ratchet assembly is made up of R1, R2, R3, and R4. Look at the exploded drawing to see how the ratchet is assembled. Glue all of the pieces together. After the assembly has dried, bore out the center with a ⁹⁄₆₄"-diameter bit. Mount the GW and ratchet assembly onto the frame with a spacer between the ratchet assembly and F2. Install the hour wheel pinion on this axle in front of F1.

Step 14: Assemble the Second Wheel (2W) and the Third Wheel (3W). These wheels have the pinions glued in place on the front of the wheel. The 2W pinion has eight leaves, and the 3W pinion has seven leaves. The side view on the exploded drawing shows the spacers made from ⁵⁄₃₂"-diameter brass tubing that go on the axles. Note how the pallet axle has the spacers mounted on it. The other axles will be similar.

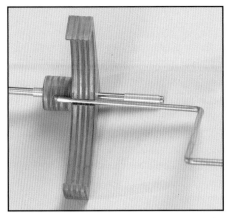

Step 15: Glue the Pallets (P) and the Pallet Collar (PC) together.
Drill a 3/32"-diameter hole into the bottom of the collar for the crutch. Lay the 3/32"-diameter brass rod on the crutch pattern and bend accordingly. Install the pallets onto the frame, and insert the crutch through the hole in the frame (F2) and into the pallet collar. This should be a tight fit. Add a few drops of shellac to secure the crutch in the pallet slot. At this time, go back and insert a couple of drops of shellac into the holes between the leaves of the pinions. This will adhere the pinions to the axles.

Mount the Clock and Assemble the Pendulum

Step 16: Hang the clock. Find a stud on the wall, and drill in the hanger bolt in a spot where the clock will hang about 6" above you. Slip the clock part WA onto the bolt. Be sure the anchor pins are inserted into the ends of ribs 4 and 8. Lay a small level between ribs 4 and 8, and level the clock. Mark where the anchor pins are touching the wall, and drill 1/8"-diameter holes for them. This will anchor the clock into the wall.

Step 17: Assemble the pendulum rod. The pendulum rod is made up of a pendulum spring, pendulum top (PT), pendulum bottom (PB) and a 3/8"-diameter x 36"-long dowel. Make the spring out of steel fishing leader, using the spring-bending jig. Attach the

spring to the PT with a cotter key or a brad. The dowel is attached to the PT and the PB with a 1/16"-diameter pin made by cutting both ends off a brad. The PB has a slot for the machine screw as shown in the illustration. Screw the rating nut onto the machine screw to thread it.

Step 18: Assemble the bob.
Apply glue to the back of B1, and press it onto B2. Fill in the gaps on B1 with lead shot. Apply glue to B1, and press B3 onto it. Clamp the three together, and allow the glue to dry. Trim the bob as shown on the drawings. This will give you a clean edge. Install the bob onto the end of the pendulum rod by threading the machine screw through the hole in the bottom of the bob. Thread the rating nut onto the machine screw to hold it in place. Insert a pin (made from a 1/16" brad) into the post on rib 12 and hang the pendulum onto the post as shown on the assembly diagram.

Step 19: Install the weight and counterweight. Make a noose knot (see page 124) on one end of the

fishing string, and insert it into R2, bringing the other end through the noose. The string in the front will be for the weight, and the string in the back for the counterweight. Wind the front string counterclockwise, and then hang the weight on the end. Hang the counterweight on the back string. As the weight comes down, the counterweight will wind up onto R2. To rewind the clock, simply pull down the counterweight.

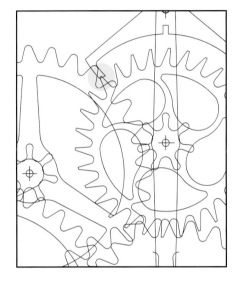

Tweak the Clock for Ultimate Performance

Step 20: Put the clock into beat.
Look at the diagram of the clock above. Notice the yellow highlight around the entrance pallet where it rests on the escape wheel's tooth. With the weight hanging and the pendulum not moving, this is the position in which the pallet and tooth should be. If not, bend the crutch until you have attained this position. Move the pendulum either way about 2", and release it. The clock should run. Listen to the tick-tock of the pallets. They should be beating in an even rhythm. If not, bend the crutch either way until you get an even tick-tock. Run the clock for a week, making adjustments as needed. You may need to sand the teeth or leaves a bit to help the clock run smoothly.

How the Wooden Gear Clock Works

The clock is powered by the weight. As the weight drops, the counterweight rises. The weight is connected to the ratchet assembly, which is connected to the great wheel (GW). The energy from the GW travels backward through the clock to the pendulum and forwards to the hour wheel (HW).

Notice the thickness of the GW. This added weight gives it additional power to turn the pinion on the second wheel (2W). The 2W is thinner and weighs much less than the GW, making it easier to turn. The 2W turns the pinion on the third wheel (3W), which is the thinnest wheel, and thus takes even less energy to turn. The 3W turns the escape wheel pinion which turns the escape wheel (EW).

The function of the EW is to keep the pallets (P) moving. The pallets are connected to the crutch that propels the pendulum side to side. The weight has about 3lbs of lead shot in it. Only about 1oz of this weight is

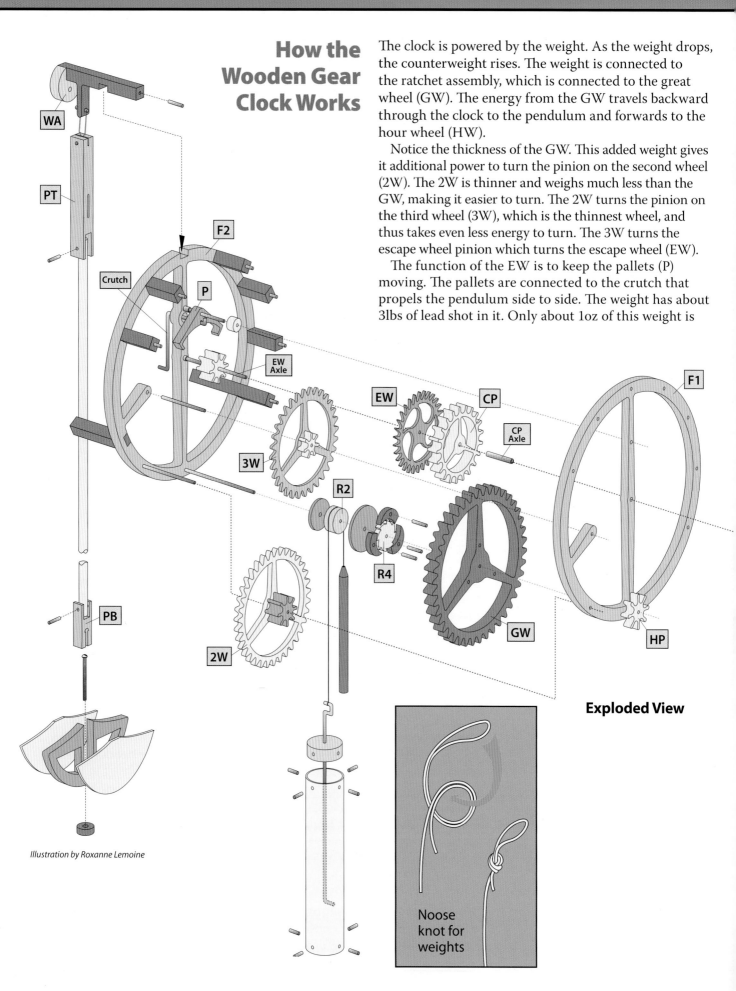

Exploded View

WA, PT, Crutch, F2, P, EW Axle, EW, CP, CP Axle, F1, 3W, R2, R4, GW, HP, 2W, PB

Noose knot for weights

Illustration by Roxanne Lemoine

transferred to the EW. So you can see the importance of reducing the size of each wheel. A heavier wheel will turn a smaller wheel much easier than one of equal size. The pendulum regulates the speed of the clock. This is a "1 meter" pendulum that swings one second at a time.

While the hands are all positioned on the same axle, they reside on different tubes or axles and move independently according to the movement of the pinion or wheel that shares the same axle or tube. The EW axle is made from ⅛"-diameter steel rod and it slides through the canon pinion (CP) tube/axle. The second hand is mounted on the EW axle. The CP is turned by the GW, and its axle is made from ⁵⁄₃₂"-diameter tubing. The minute hand is mounted on the CP axle/tube. The HW is turned by the hour pinion (HP) which shares an axle with the GW. The HW axle is made from ³⁄₁₆"-diameter tubing, which slides over the CP tube/axle. The hour hand is mounted on the HW axle/tube. You need to study this very closely and look at the drawings to fully understand this design.

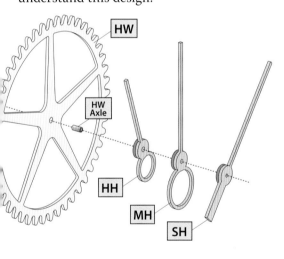

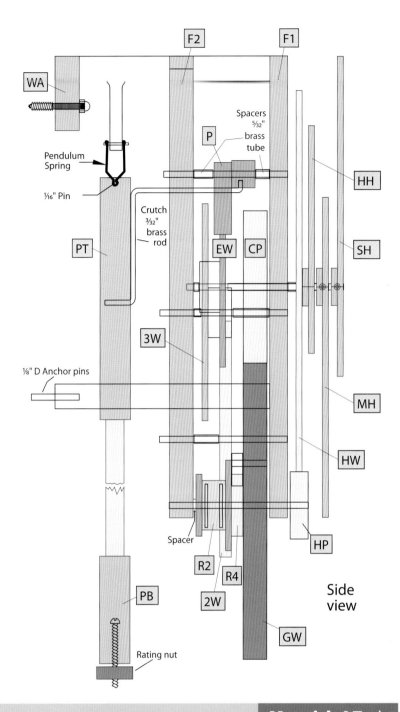

Side view

Materials & Tools

Materials:
- Baltic birch plywood:
  - ¾" x 1½" x 1½"
  - 2 pieces ½" x 12" x 12"
  - ⅜" x 12" x 12"
  - ¼" x 12" x 12"
  - 2 pieces ⅛" x 12" x 12"
- 5 pounds of #7½ lead shot
- 12' of 20-pound test braided fishing line
- 7" x 1½"-inside diameter thin-wall PVC pipe
- #8-32 x 2"-long machine screw

- Wood dowels: ⅜"-diameter x 36"-long & ⅛"-diameter x 36"-long
- 3 each ⅛"-diameter set screws with corresponding hex (allen) wrench
- ⅛"-diameter x 24" stainless steel rod
- ³⁄₁₆"-diameter x 12" brass tube
- ⁵⁄₃₂"-diameter x 12" brass tube
- ⅛"-diameter x 12" brass rod
- ³⁄₃₂" x 12" brass rod (crutch)
- Spray adhesive

- Steel fishing leader (pendulum spring)
- ¹⁄₁₆" brads
- Wood glue (I use Gorilla Glue)
- ³⁄₁₆"-diameter by 1½"-long hanger bolt with matching acorn nut
- Assorted grits of sandpaper up to 400-grit
- Aniline dye colors of choice
- Denatured alcohol
- Shellac or varnish
- Small piece of leather (for 3 plugs)

Tools:
- #1 reverse-tooth blades or blades of choice
- Assorted small clamps
- Small, round file
- Hacksaw or rotary power carver with carbide cutting disc
- Drill
- Brad-point drill bits: ¹⁄₁₆", ⅛", ³⁄₁₆", and ⅜" diameter
- Drill bits: ⁹⁄₆₄" and ⁵⁄₃₂" diameter

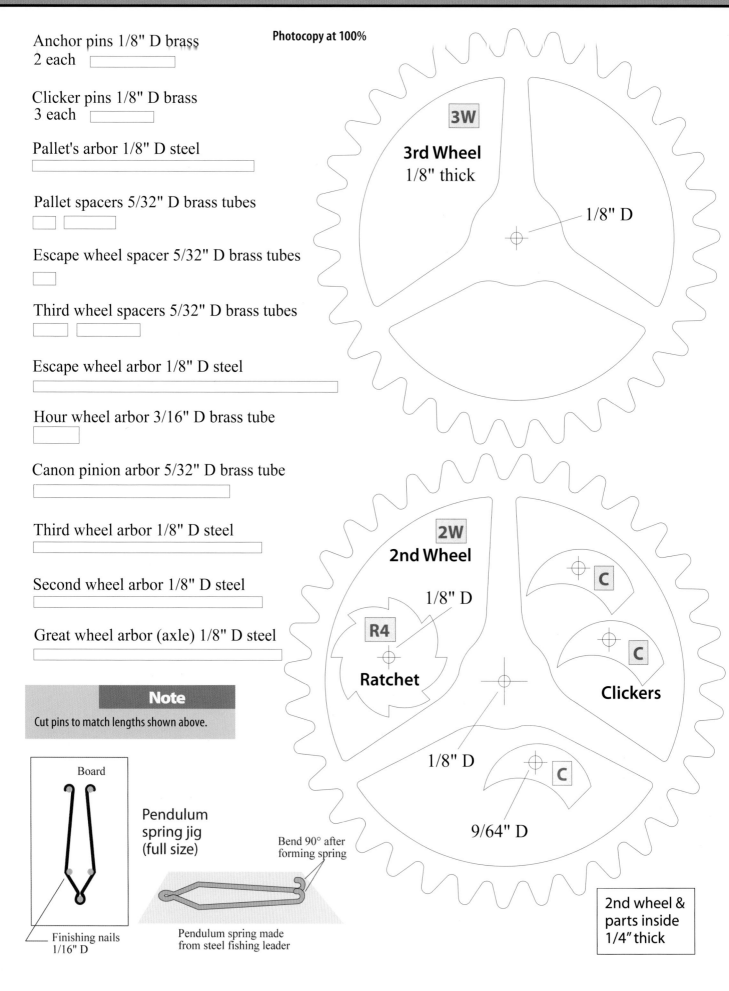

Anchor pins 1/8" D brass
2 each

Clicker pins 1/8" D brass
3 each

Pallet's arbor 1/8" D steel

Pallet spacers 5/32" D brass tubes

Escape wheel spacer 5/32" D brass tubes

Third wheel spacers 5/32" D brass tubes

Escape wheel arbor 1/8" D steel

Hour wheel arbor 3/16" D brass tube

Canon pinion arbor 5/32" D brass tube

Third wheel arbor 1/8" D steel

Second wheel arbor 1/8" D steel

Great wheel arbor (axle) 1/8" D steel

Photocopy at 100%

3W
3rd Wheel
1/8" thick

1/8" D

2W
2nd Wheel

1/8" D

R4

Ratchet

C

C

Clickers

1/8" D

C

9/64" D

2nd wheel &
parts inside
1/4" thick

Note

Cut pins to match lengths shown above.

Board

**Pendulum
spring jig
(full size)**

Bend 90° after
forming spring

Finishing nails
1/16" D

Pendulum spring made
from steel fishing leader

Photocopy at 100%

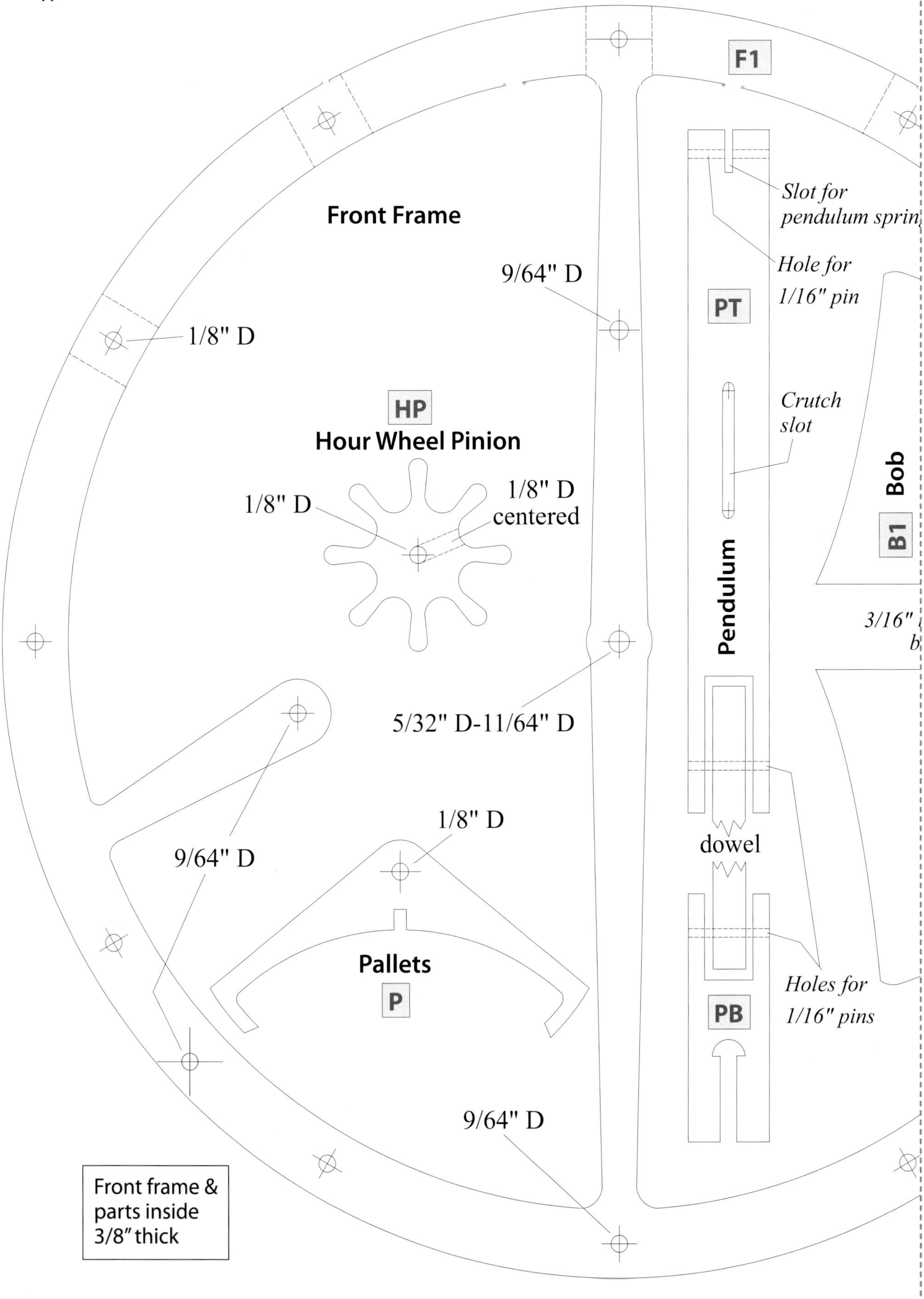
F1
Front Frame
1/8" D
9/64" D
PT
Slot for
pendulum sprin
Hole for
1/16" pin
Crutch
slot
Bob
B1
HP
Hour Wheel Pinion
1/8" D
1/8" D
centered
Pendulum
3/16"
b
5/32" D-11/64" D
9/64" D
1/8" D
dowel
Pallets
P
PB
Holes for
1/16" pins
9/64" D

Front frame & parts inside 3/8" thick

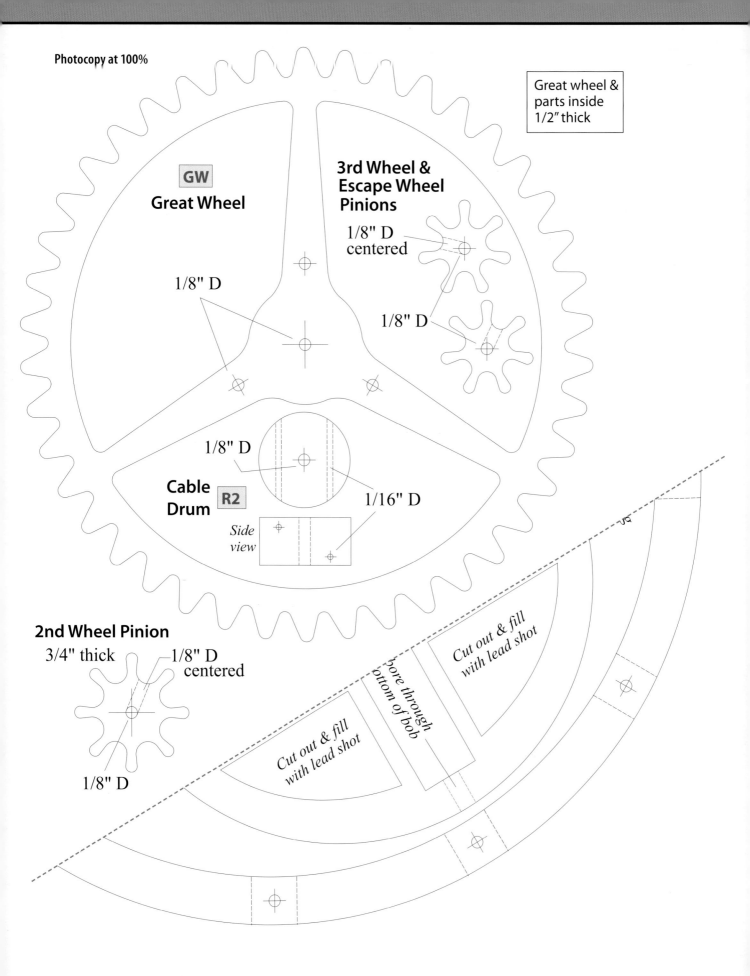

Great wheel &
parts inside
1/2" thick

GW
Great Wheel

**3rd Wheel &
Escape Wheel
Pinions**

1/8" D
centered

1/8" D

1/8" D

1/8" D

**Cable
Drum** R2

1/16" D

*Side
view*

2nd Wheel Pinion

3/4" thick   1/8" D
centered

1/8" D

*Cut out & fill
with lead shot*

*Cut out & fill
with lead shot*

*bore through
bottom of bob*

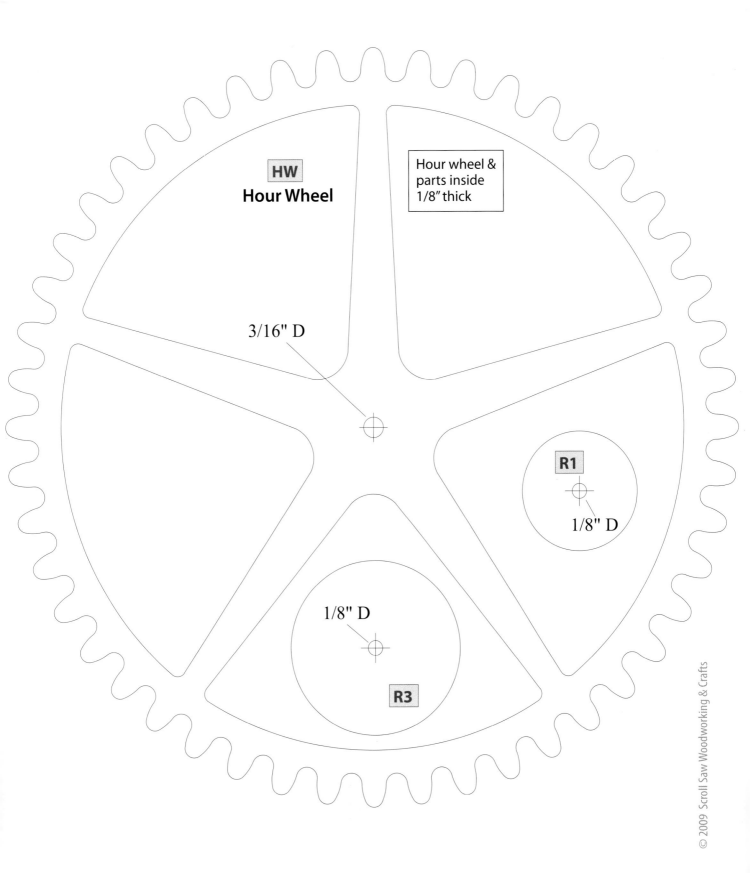

HW
Hour Wheel

Hour wheel &
parts inside
1/8" thick

3/16" D

R1

1/8" D

1/8" D

R3

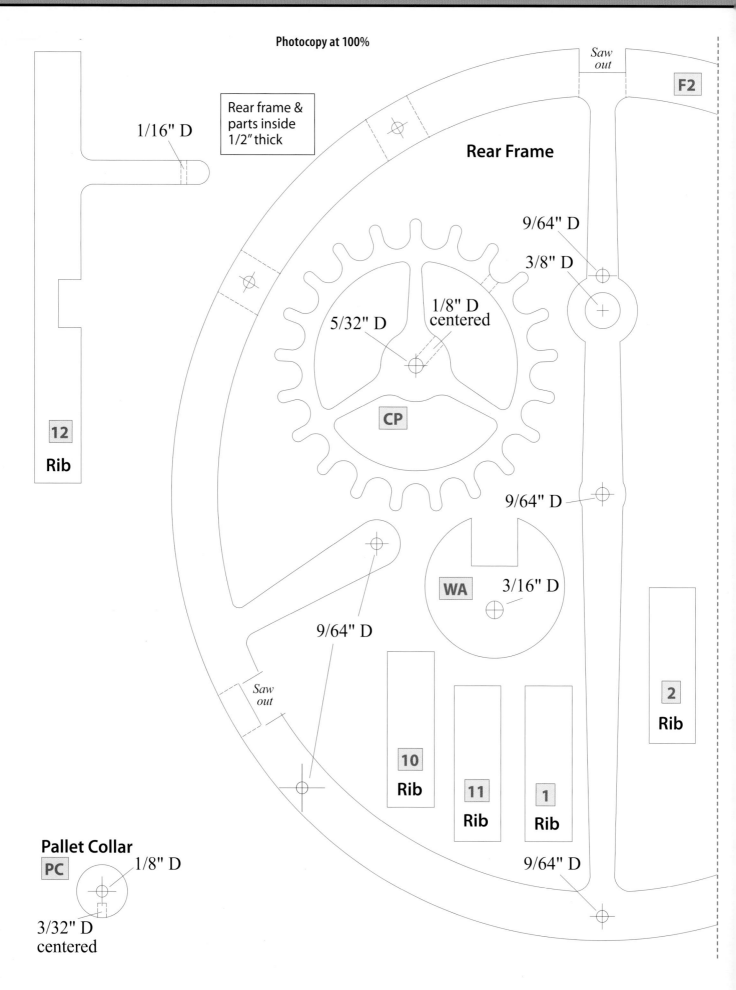

1/16" D

Rear frame &
parts inside
1/2" thick

Rear Frame

F2

Saw
out

9/64" D

3/8" D

1/8" D
centered

5/32" D

CP

9/64" D

9/64" D

WA

3/16" D

12

Rib

2

Rib

9/64" D

Saw
out

10

Rib

11

Rib

1

Rib

9/64" D

Pallet Collar

PC

1/8" D

3/32" D
centered

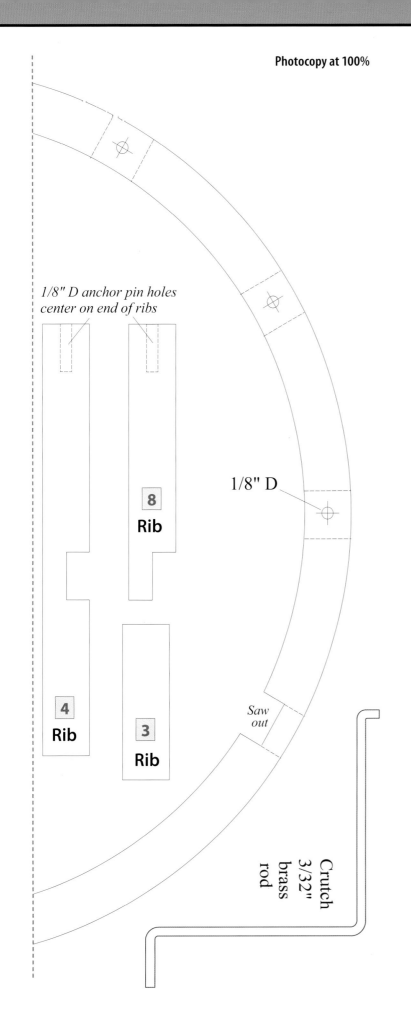

1/8" D anchor pin holes center on end of ribs

8

Rib

4

Rib

3

Rib

1/8" D

Saw out

Crutch
3/32"
brass
rod

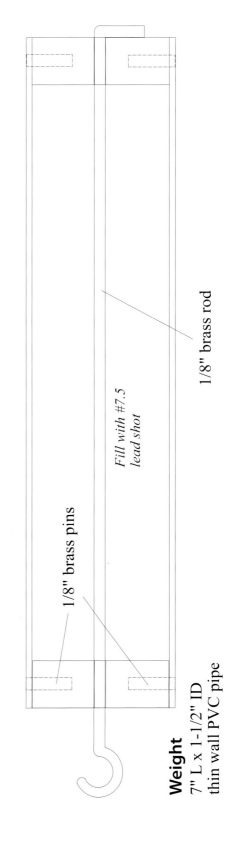

1/8" brass rod

Fill with #7.5 lead shot

1/8" brass pins

Weight
7" L x 1-1/2" ID
thin wall PVC pipe

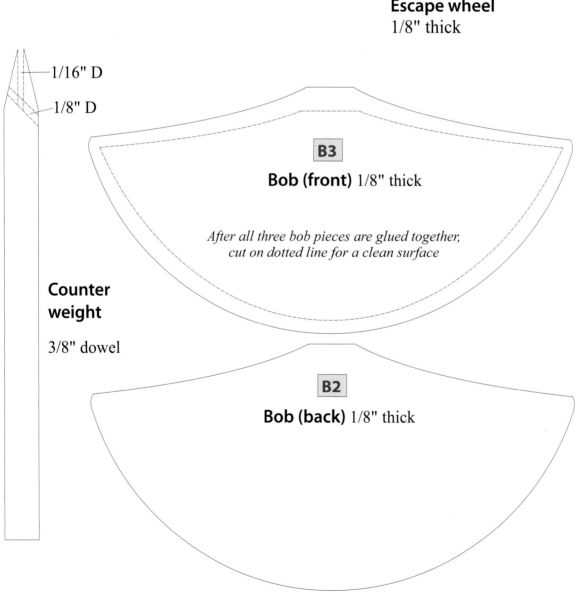

1/8" D

End Plugs
1/2" thick

1/8" D

EW
Escape wheel
1/8" thick

1/16" D

1/8" D

B3

Bob (front) 1/8" thick

After all three bob pieces are glued together,
cut on dotted line for a clean surface

Counter
weight

3/8" dowel

B2

Bob (back) 1/8" thick

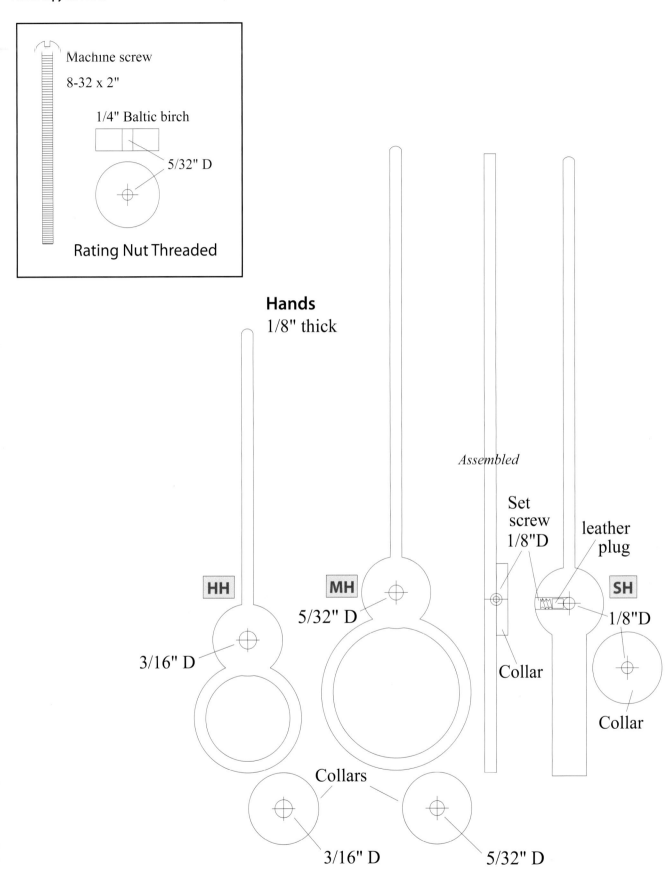

Machine screw

8-32 x 2"

1/4" Baltic birch

5/32" D

Rating Nut Threaded

Hands
1/8" thick

Assembled

Set
screw
1/8"D

leather
plug

HH

MH

5/32" D

SH

1/8"D

3/16" D

Collar

Collar

Collars

3/16" D

5/32" D

© 2009 Scroll Saw Woodworking & Crafts

"In Flight" Waterfowl Clock

Give your work a unique look with a distinctive screen accent

By Tim Andrews

This clock is relatively easy to scroll. What makes it unique is the black screen I use as a backing. The screen, which is simply fiberglass window screen, gives the project an entirely different look.

When selecting wood for the project, I look for a piece with an interesting grain to enhance the pattern. Many lumber stores have oak plywood in 24" x 24" sizes. I cut this down to 12" x 12" and sand both sides with 220-grit sandpaper.

APPLYING A SPRAY FINISH	TIP

I spray the back first, paying close attention to the crevices. If I become overzealous with the first coat, and it starts to run, it won't be so apparent on the back of the project.

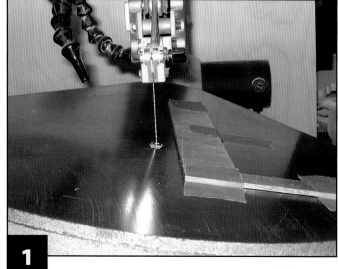

1 **Cut the bottom edge of the blank at a 10° angle.** This angle is easily cut with a table saw or miter saw or can be made by locking your scroll saw table at a 10° angle. Tape a straight edge (I use a metal square) to the table so that it is parallel to the side of the blade. With the back of the project facing up, place the bottom edge of the wood against the straight edge. Cut the side off with a #5 reverse-tooth blade. You want the stock to be slightly shorter on the back so the project leans back when finished. Cut a 10° bevel on one edge of a piece of scrap. With the bevel along the straight side, cut out a semi-circle for the base. It should be about 4½" along the straight side with a 2¾" radius. After cutting, return the table to level, and check to make sure your blade is square to the table.

Cutting the design

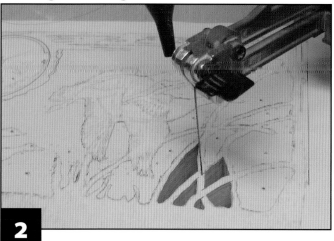

2 **Cut out the ducks, reeds, and clouds with a #5 blade.** Cut the veining and details with a #1 reverse-tooth blade. Use a ¹⁄₁₆"-diameter bit for the blade entry holes and the ducks' eyes, but don't drill the eyes the whole way through.

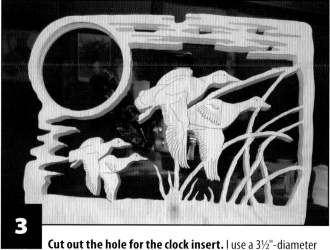

3 **Cut out the hole for the clock insert.** I use a 3½"-diameter clock insert that requires a 3"-diameter hole. Cut inside the hole and sand it to fit your specific clock. Sand the entire project to remove any burrs or rough edges.

4 **Attach the base.** Lay the work front-down on a flat surface. Apply wood glue sparingly to both surfaces, and allow it to dry for a minute. Join the pieces and match the edges so the base and the bottom edge of the main piece are one smooth surface. Allow the glue to dry.

5 **Apply your finish of choice.** If using a stain, apply that first. I use clear fast-drying polyurethane. To suspend the project, hook a wire coat hanger through the clock insert hole. Apply three coats allowing each to dry before applying the next. Let this cure for a couple days.

6 **Add the fiberglass screen to the back.** Trace the outline of the finished clock onto the screen. Cut ⅛" inside the line, and glue the screen to the back of the clock. Cut a hole in the screen, and insert the clock to finish the project.

Materials & Tools

Materials:
- ¾" x 12" x 12" oak plywood or wood of choice
- Sandpaper, 220 grit
- Temporary bond spray adhesive
- Fiberglass screen
- Fast-drying polyurethane or finish of choice
- 3½" (90mm)-diameter clock insert with corresponding battery
- Tape of choice
- Wood glue

Tools:
- #1 and #5 reverse-tooth scroll saw blades or blades of choice
- Square or metal straight edge
- Miter saw or table saw (optional)

Photocopy at 100%

The Lang Clock

Easy-to-cut clock is a beautiful addition to any home

By Dale Helgerson

A friend inquired about a clock after seeing some of my scrolling. She looked at photos and thumbed through several catalogs, looking for a clock that suited her tastes. They were all "too frilly" and "too fancy," so I designed something specifically for her.

With paper, pencil, straight edge, and compass, I began drawing ideas. When I delivered the clock to her, she loved it. This clock is named after her; after all, she inspired me to design it!

The Lang Clock is best made by stack-cutting two clocks at once, using contrasting woods. By saving the cutouts from one type of wood and inserting them into the other, you can create two attractive clocks with very little waste.

The project uses mainly straight cuts and gradual curves. This makes it easy enough for the beginner, yet elegant enough for the skilled scroller. It can be cut using pin-end blades, something that very few of the larger clock patterns are capable of.

The clocks pictured were cut using red oak and walnut, but any two contrasting woods will look equally impressive. Try experimenting with different combinations to personalize your timepiece.

Cutting the Clocks

Start by cutting the pieces to size, using the materials list and cutting diagram as guides (see page 140, 142). I use a table saw and a miter saw. Cut each piece to size in both red oak and walnut. Attach the contrasting pieces together to stack cut on the scroll saw. I tape the edges together with masking tape, but double-sided tape works as well. I do not suggest using nails or brads, because the thin hardwood splits easily.

Apply clear packaging tape to the top of the stack. Apply spray adhesive to the back of the pattern, and align the corner of the pattern with the bottom corner of the stack. Press the pattern firmly onto the taped surface. The tape lubricates the blade and makes it easier to remove the pattern.

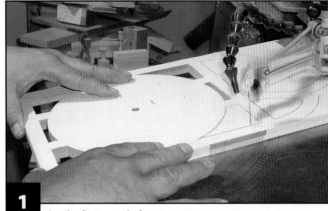

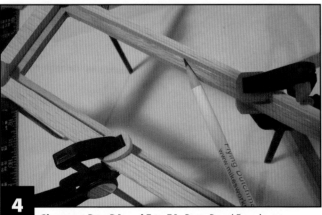

1 **Cut the first round of parts.** Drill a ¹³⁄₃₂"-diameter hole for the clock movement on part A. On parts A, B, N and NA, drill ¹⁄₁₆"-diameter blade entry holes and cut the frets. DO NOT cut the perimeters at this time. Cut the corner notches on part B. Save the inside cutouts from parts B and NA for later use.

2 **Glue the parts together.** Separate the stacks and remove the patterns from B and NA only. Apply a light coat of yellow carpenter's glue to the top sides of parts B and NA. Matching the woods, line up the top edges of A and B, and the bottom edges of N and NA. Clamp until dry. The arches on A and N are thicker and will create a lip for the inlays. Repeat for the second clock.

3 **Cut the second round of parts.** Drill the blade entry holes as close to a corner as possible. Cut parts C, D, DA, E, EA, F, G, H, K, L, M, and O. Save the cutouts from parts DA and EA. Separate all of the stacks and remove the patterns. Lightly sand all the pieces. Group the parts according to wood species with the exception of part O. The oak O will be assembled with the walnut clock.

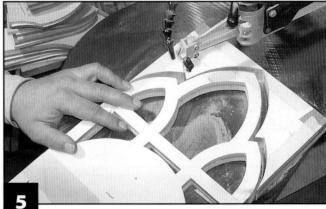

4 **Glue part D to DA and E to EA.** Parts D and E are longer than DA and EA. Line these parts up with the overhang at the top and the thicker long side to the left of one piece and the right of the opposing piece. Matching the woods, glue part D to DA and E to EA. Line up the bottom edge and side and clamp until dry. Note that you are creating a lip for the inlay as you did in Step 2.

5 **Cut the outer arches.** Stack both N/NA assemblies together. Stack both A/B assemblies together. For the A/B stack, use ¼"-thick material to shim between the two pieces at the lower end and on the bottom so it sits flat on your saw table. Secure the stacks with masking tape and cut the outer profiles. I use a #7 FD-SR blade. Remove the patterns and sand lightly.

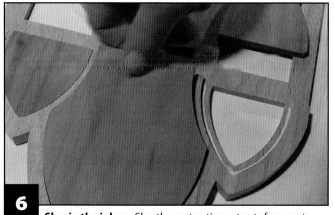

6 **Glue in the inlays.** Glue the contrasting cut outs from parts B, DA, EA, and NA into the openings. (I use Aleene's quick dry tacky glue). Check for any glue squeeze-out.

Assembling the Clocks

Clock assembly is straightforward. Use the exploded drawing on the following page as a guide.

Step 1: **Test fit the pieces.** Align the sides (D and E) and front (A/B) together with C, G, and I to be sure the edges line up nicely. Slight variations of wood thickness may make it necessary to trim parts C–G and I, so the corners of D and E meet nicely with part A/B. Note that the sides will fit into the notches on B and the wider long side is toward the back.

Step 2: **Attach part I to part C.** The beveled edge should face the inside of the clock. Use wire brads and glue for added strength; the clock hangs from the bevel.

Step 3: **Attach one side.** Line up one side (D or E) with the back of A/B, sliding the piece up into the notch on B. Line up C beneath B and drill small pilot holes through A/B into C. The pilot holes help to prevent the wood from splitting—choose spots where the wood is least likely to split. Glue and clamp the side (D or E) and C to A/B. Use ¾" brads through the pilot holes to strengthen that joint as it will bear the weight of the clock.

Step 4: **Attach the floor and opposite side.** Line up G flush with the bottom of the first side and attach the remaining side panel (D or E). Glue and clamp until dry.

Step 5: **Attach part O.** Be sure to use the contrasting wood and place O inside the clock case. Use a pencil to mark the cut-out circle location on the inside of A/B. Remove O and apply a bead of glue approximately ¼" outside your pencil line and along the inner edges of the case. Insert O back in the case. Run a bead of glue (like a bead of weld) around the outer edge of O, as well as around the inside of the circle. Weigh down or clamp the piece to hold it in place.

7 **Cut parts I and J to size.** Bevel one edge as shown on the plan. Drill and countersink a ⅛"-diameter hole where indicated on part J. This will be used to mount your clock onto the wall.

Step 6: **Test fit the shelf to the lower portion of the clock.** The notch in F should fit snugly over the sides of part N/NA. Widen the slot if needed.

Step 7: **Glue the main base together.** Glue and clamp H ½" down and parallel to the flat edge of N/NA. H should be centered on N/NA to allow you to attach L and M flush with the sides of N/NA. It is best to dry fit these pieces first in case any adjustments are needed. Glue the base sides (L and M) in place with the straight edge flush with H and the longer side against N/NA.

Step 8: **Attach the base fretwork front.** Glue K on top of the sides and flush with part H.

Step 9: **Sand all of the corners to a crisp, sharp point.** Putty any nail holes, if applicable.

Step 10: **Attach the shelf to the clock base.** Glue and clamp F to the lower clock assembly.

Step 11: **Assemble the two sections.** Line up the pendulum opening, and look straight down the corner to ensure proper alignment. Use two #6 x 1¼"-long wood screws and glue to hold the halves together. Insert the screws through G into the base assembly.

Step 12: **Apply your finish of choice.** I apply one coat of Danish oil, followed by four coats of clear, semi-gloss wood finish. Sand between coats with fine-grit sandpaper.

Step 13: **Install the clock movement.** A 7" to 8"-diameter dial looks best. I used a 7⅞" dial on the clocks shown. Screw part J to the wall, with the bevel up and toward the wall. Align the bevel on I and J to hang up your clock.

A - Front overlay
B - Crown inlay/underlay
C - Top (not on pattern)
D & E - Body side overlay
DA & EA - Body side inlay/underlay
F - Base shelf
G - Upper floor
H - Lower floor
I - Hanger strip
J - Wall hanger strip
K - Base fretwork front
L & M - Base fretwork sides
N - Base overlay
NA - Base inlay/underlay
O - Underlay body panel

▨ - Oak
▨ - Walnut

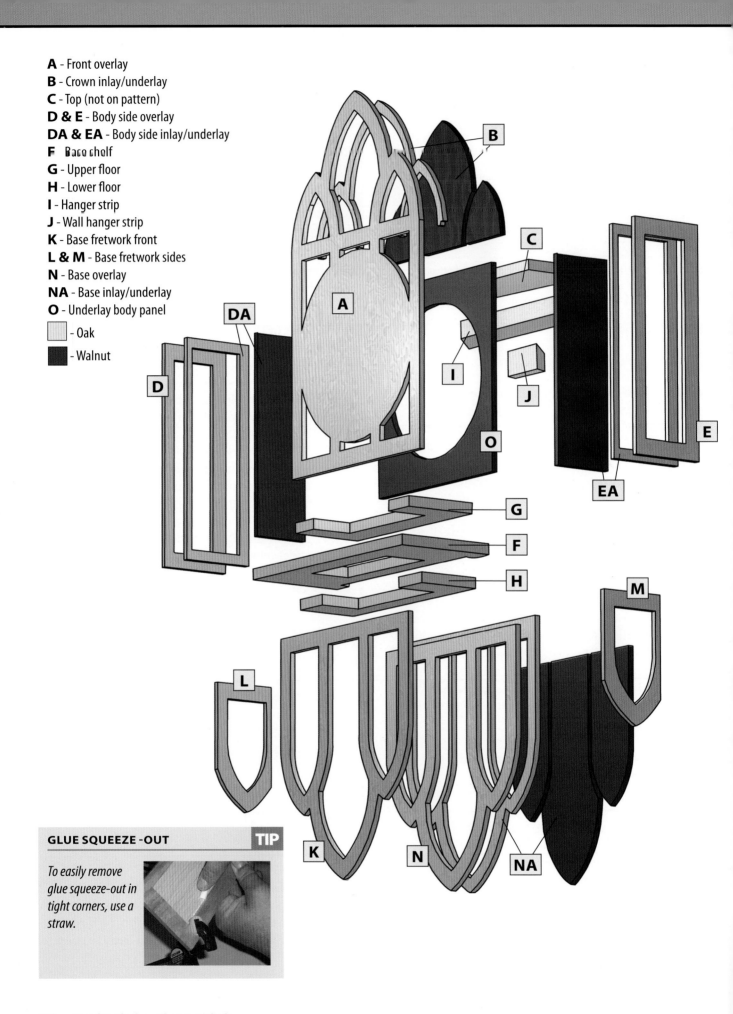

GLUE SQUEEZE-OUT   **TIP**

To easily remove glue squeeze-out in tight corners, use a straw.

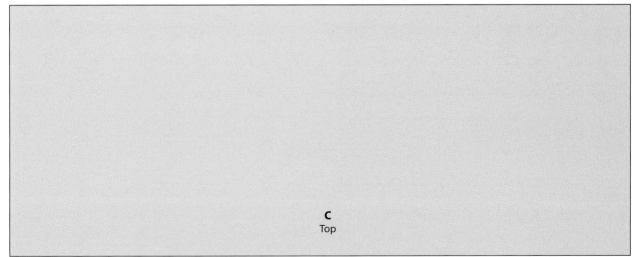

Materials:

2 pieces of contrasting woods like oak and walnut in these dimensions:
- ¼" x 10" x 17⅝" (A)
- ¼" x 10" x 6¾" (B)
- ½" x 3½" x 9" (C) (no pattern)
- ¼" x 3½" x 11" (D)
- ¼" x 3½" x 10⅞" (DA)
- ¼" x 3½" x 11" (E)
- ¼" x 3½" x 10⅞" (EA)
- ½" x 4¾" x 12" (F)
- ½" x 3½" x 9" (G)
- ½" x 3" x 9½" (H)
- ½" x 1¼" x 9" (I)
- ½" x 1¼" x 2½" (J)
- ¼" x 10" x 11¾" (K)
- ¼" x 3" x 6⅛" (L)
- ¼" x 3" x 6⅛" (M)
- ¼" x 10" x 12½" (N)
- ¼" x 10" x 12½" (NA)
- ¼" x 8⅞" x 9⅞" (O)
- Clear packaging tape
- Small brads (¾" long)
- 2 each #6 x 1¼" wood screws
- Spray adhesive
- Glue of choice
- Finish (I use Danish Oil and Deft clear wood finish)

Clock Movement Parts:
- Hermle chime with pendulum
- 6" lyre attachment
- 7⅞"-diameter Arabic Elegant dial
- Hands (3⅛"-long minute) black
- Pendulum bob
- Pendulum rod (request Single Hook) *This movement requires the speaker mount.*

Tools:
- Table saw and miter saw (optional)
- Drill (press or handheld)
- Clamps for assembly

- Various drill bits, including ¹³⁄₃₂" and ¹⁄₁₆" diameter
- Various scroll saw blades (I use #5 and #7 reverse-tooth blades)
- Screwdriver for mounting movement (if needed)
- Hammer if using small brads during assembly

USING PINNED BLADES   `TIP`

Finally, a clock that can be made with pinned blades! By carefully placing your blade entry holes in parts DA, EA, and NA you can cut this clock on a saw that requires pin-end blades. Using a ³⁄₁₆"-diameter drill bit, drill your blade entry holes right on the pattern line for the area to be cut on parts DA, EA, and NA. All other openings to be cut should be drilled in the waste areas as you normally would. Once assembled, your blade-entry holes will only be visible from the backside of your clock.

C
Top

Photocopy at 135%

Cutting Diagram

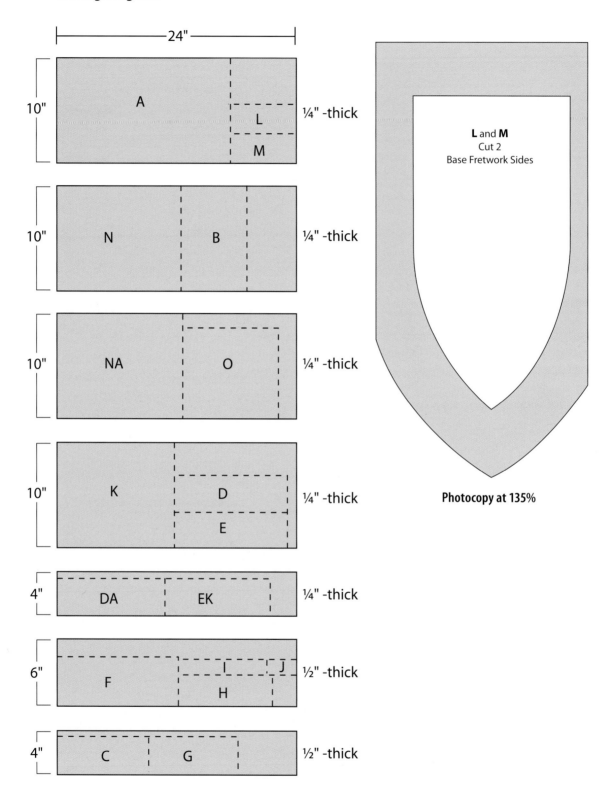

|←——— 24" ———→|

10" A   L   M   ¼" -thick

10" N   B   ¼" -thick

10" NA   O   ¼" -thick

10" K   D   E   ¼" -thick

4"   DA   EK   ¼" -thick

6"   F   I   J   H   ½" -thick

4"   C   G   ½" -thick

L and **M**
Cut 2
Base Fretwork Sides

Photocopy at 135%

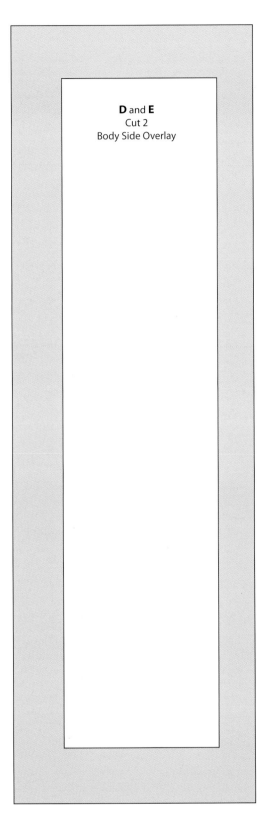

D and **E**
Cut 2
Body Side Overlay

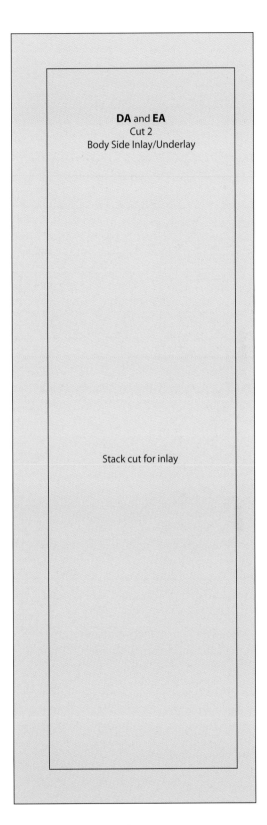

DA and **EA**
Cut 2
Body Side Inlay/Underlay

Stack cut for inlay

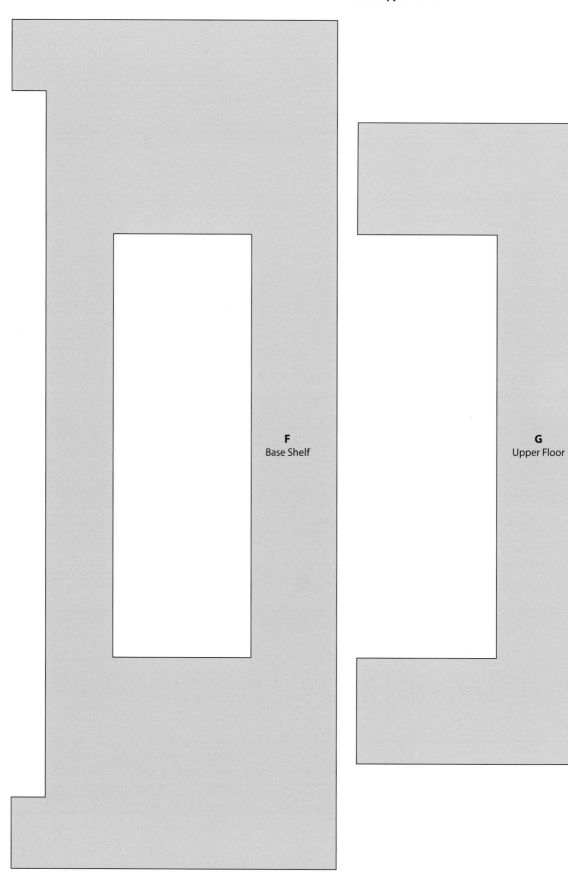

F
Base Shelf

G
Upper Floor

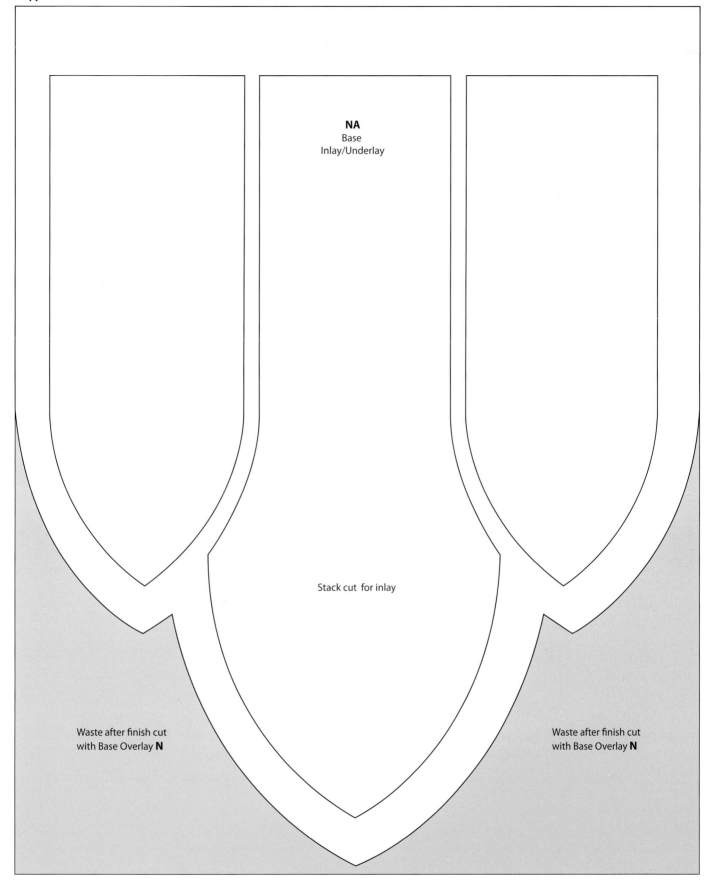

NA
Base
Inlay/Underlay

Stack cut for inlay

Waste after finish cut
with Base Overlay **N**

Waste after finish cut
with Base Overlay **N**

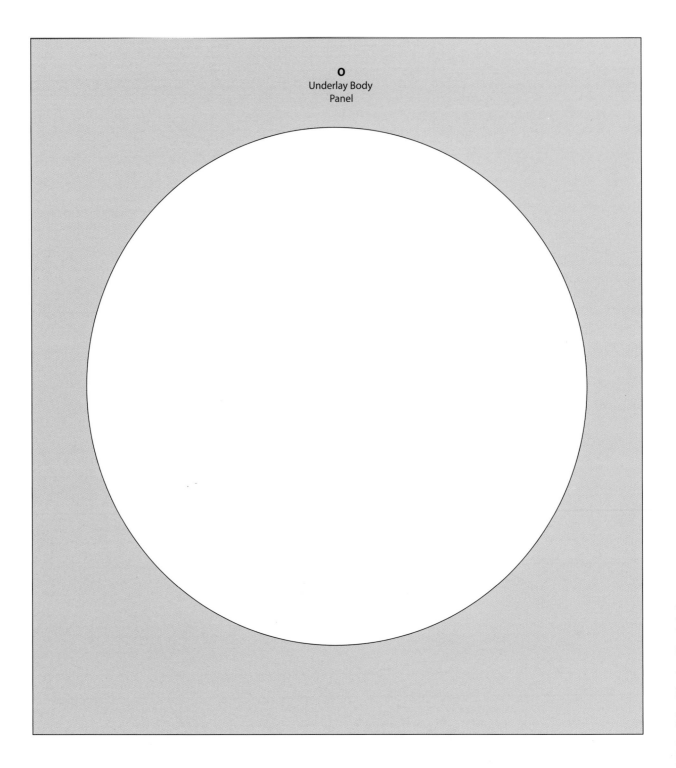

O
Underlay Body
Panel

Photocopy at 135%

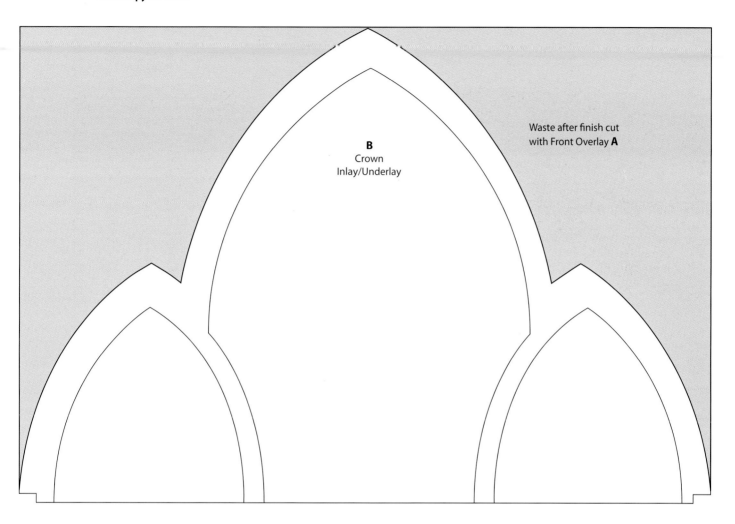

B
Crown
Inlay/Underlay

Waste after finish cut
with Front Overlay **A**

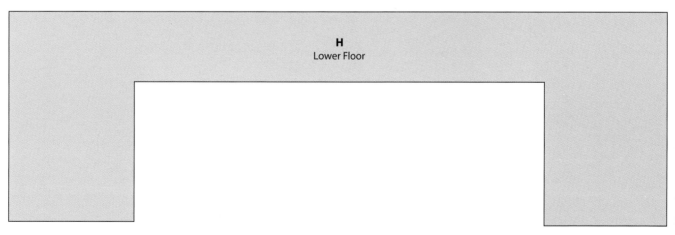

H
Lower Floor

Photocopy at 135%

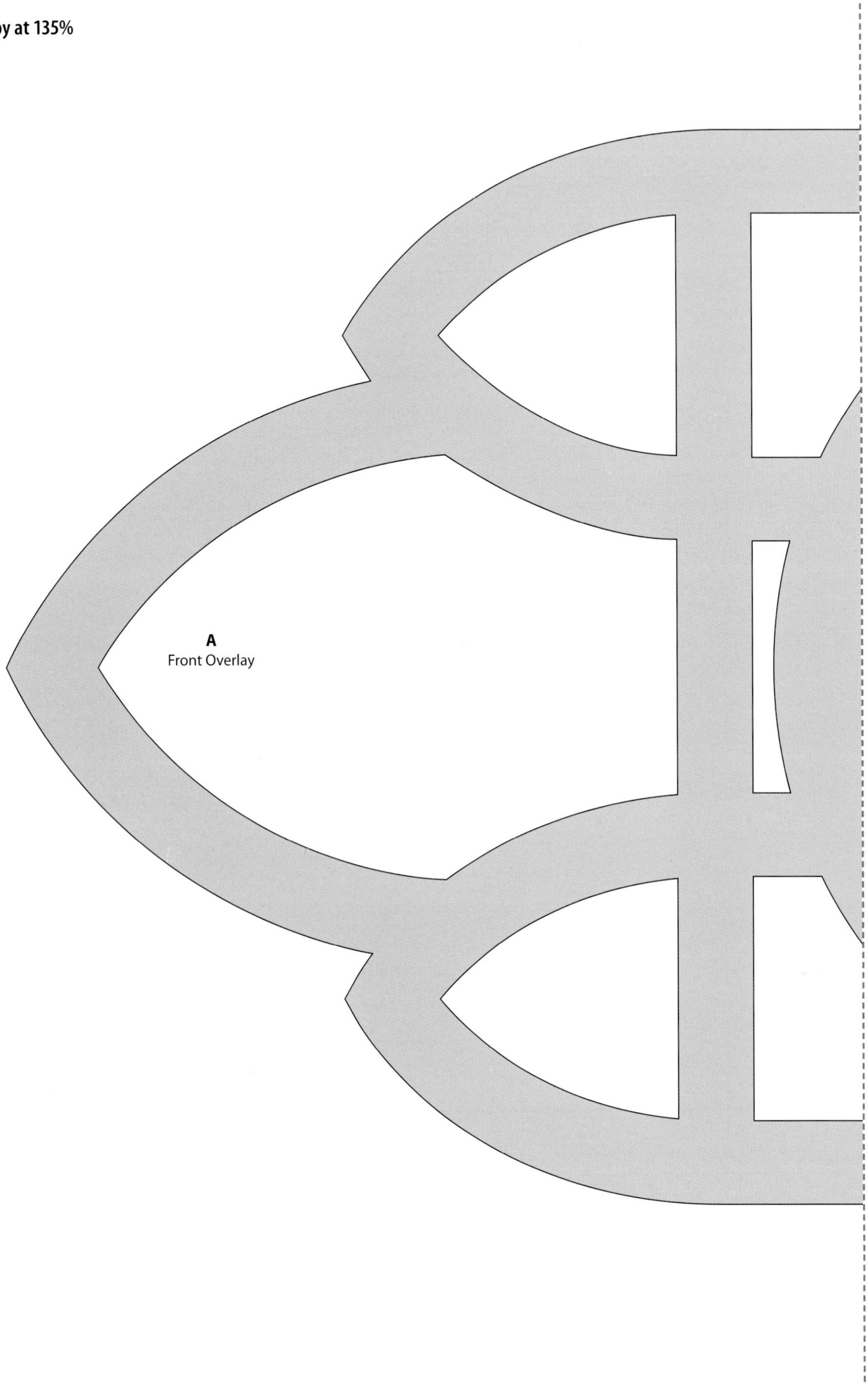

A
Front Overlay

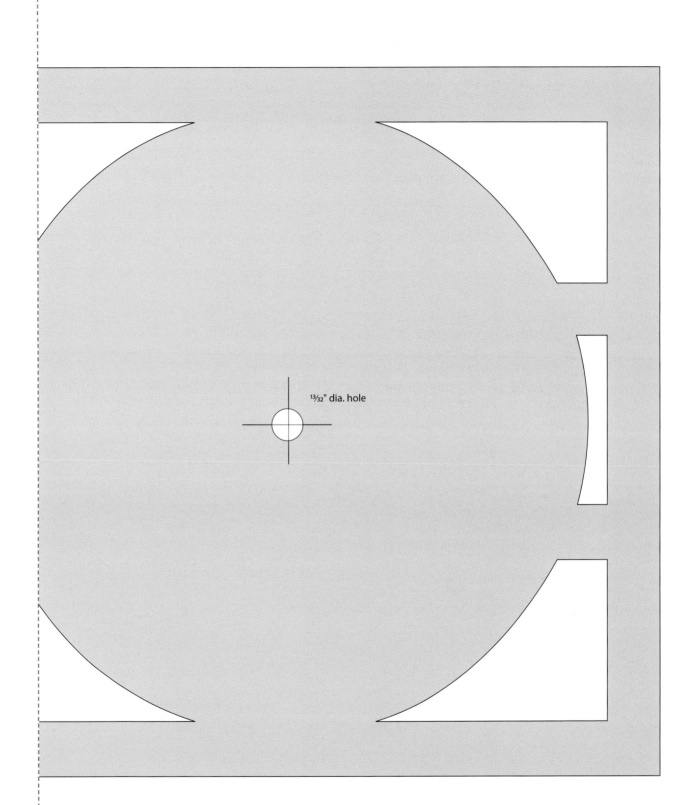

¹³⁄₃₂" dia. hole

Photocopy at 135%

N Cut Line

K Cut Line

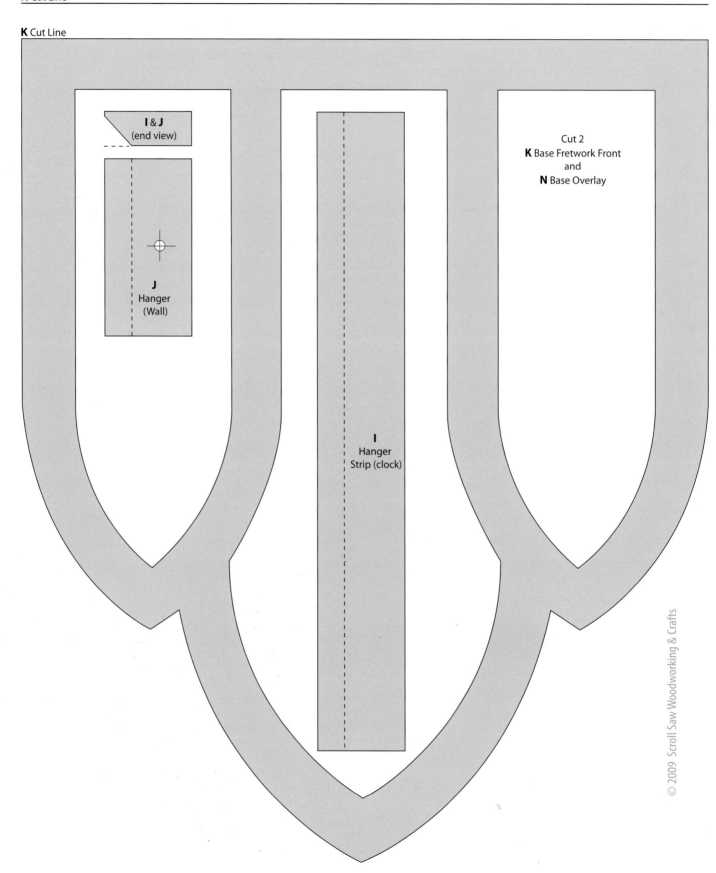

I & J
(end view)

J
Hanger
(Wall)

Cut 2
K Base Fretwork Front
and
N Base Overlay

I
Hanger
Strip (clock)

List of Contributors

Tim Andrews
Tim lives in Dickinson, TX. To see more of his work, visit his Web site.
http://etccreations.homestead.com/

Dirk Boelman
Dirk lives in Platteville, WI, and has authored several books and videos on scrolling.
www.theartfactory.com

Ed Eldridge
Ed lives in Fort Frances, Ontario, Canada, across the border from International Falls, Minnesota.
jneimp@ff.lakeheadu.ca

Steve Greytak
Steve enjoys scrolling Plexiglas, playing the accordion, and boxing.

Gary Hawkes
Gary, a fan of the rock group Pink Floyd, lives in Stagecoach, NV.

Dale Helgerson
Dale lives in Kansasville, WI and is a woodworking leader for the local 4-H club.
luckyscroller788@yahoo.com

Pedro Lopez
Pedro is a math teacher and lives in Seville, Spain. He restores historic patterns as a hobby.
www.finescrollsaw.com

Paul Meisel
Paul resides in Mound, MN, where he is an avid woodworker and designer.

Sue Mey
Sue lives in Pretoria, South Africa.
www.scrollsawartist.com

Tom Mullane
Tom is a scroller and designer who has had several articles in *Scroll Saw Woodworking & Crafts*.
www.oldgriz.biz

John A. Nelson
John, a prolific scroller and designer, contributes frequently to *Scroll Saw Woodworking & Crafts*.
www.scrollsawer.com

Dennis Simmons
Dennis, author of *Making Furniture and Dollhouses for American Girl and Other 18-Inch Dolls*, lives in Rushville, IN.
Intarsiawood@hotmail.com

Diana Thompson
Diana, who lives in Theodore, AL, is a prolific scroller and designer.
www.scrollsawinspirations.com

Marc Tovar
Marc lives in Layton, UT, and creates gear clocks.
www.wooden-clockworks.com

Kathy Wise
Kathy is known for her intarsia work. She lives in Yale, MI.
www.kathywise.com

Index

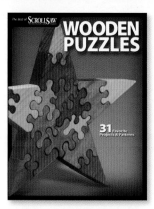

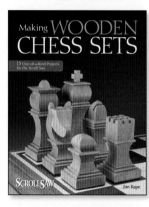
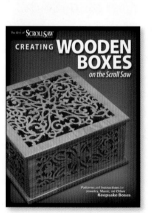
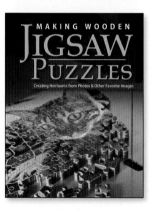